# Green Building Envelopes –

THE LATEST IN
ECO-FRIENDLY
ARCHITECTURE

Sibylle Kramer

# Green Building Envelopes –

## THE LATEST IN ECO-FRIENDLY ARCHITECTURE

BRAUN

# Content


6 Preface

8 **Shiroiya Hotel**
Sou Fujimoto Architects

12 **Maggie's Yorkshire**
Heatherwick studio

16 **Bunker St. Pauli**
Landschaftsarchitektur+
Holzapfel-Herziger & Benesch

20 **Villa M**
Triptyque

24 **The Prow at Expedia Group**
Aidlin Darling Design

28 **ASI Reisen Offices**
Snøhetta

32 **Tony Fruit Office**
TAA Design

36 **Library in the Earth**
Hiroshi Nakamura & NAP

40 **Urban Forest**
Koichi Takada Architects

44 **Tainan Market**
MVRDV

48 **Foundation for Polish Science Headquarters**
FAAB Architektura

52 **Office for Trees**
Pham Huu Son Architects

56 **FENDI Factory**
Piuarch

60 **Dune House**
Studio Vural

64 **OLA HALE Restaurant and Bar**
CHIO Architects (Singapore)

68 **Casa Abacateiro**
Ana Ruivo, Baixo Impacto Arquitetura

72 **Jipyoung Guesthouse**
Byoung Cho / BCHO Partners

76 **Green Field Factory of Karupannya**
Nakshabid Architects

80 **Grüner Pavillon**
Tom Munz Architekt*innen

84 **Hôtel De Ville Herstal**
AAFH!

88 **MIA Design Studio Office**
MIA Design Studio

92 **Factory in the Earth**
Ryuichi Ashizawa Architects & associates

96 **Regenbogenwald**
blrm Architekt*innen

100 **COAF Guest House**
Studio Paul Kaloustian

104 **Cool Shadow Office**
RATAPLAN - Architektur ZT

108 **VanDusen Botanical Garden Visitor Centre**
Perkins&Will

112 **Bi House Nha Trang**
Pham Huu Son Architects

116 **ARABELLA 26**
Aika Schluchtmann,
Schluchtmann Architekten

120 **The Coconut Club & Park**
KANOPEA ARCHITECTURE STUDIO /
T3 ARCHITECTS

124 **IKEA the good neighbour**
querkraft

128 **Touching Eden House**
Wallflower Architecture + Design

132 **Holiday home by Þingvallavatn**
KRADS

136 **Matorral**
ALH Taller

140 **Max-Planck-Institut**
Landschaftsarchitektur+
Holzapfel-Herziger & Benesch

144 **Writer's Shed**
Matt Gibson Architecture & Design

148 **DDoffice**
DDconcept Architecture

152 **Trudo Vertical Forest**
Stefano Boeri Architetti

156 **LIFE HAMBURG**
LAVA - Laboratory for Visionary
Architecture

160 **Gurdau Winery**
Aleš Fiala

164 **Yoga House**
Phạm Thanh Truyền,
Phún Bảo Long and Partners

168 **Shanghai Greenland Center**
Nikken Sekkei

173 Index

In a world suffering the impacts of climate change to an ever-greater extent, awareness of the need to rethink architecture is also growing. Traditionally, buildings were viewed as enclosed, nearly isolated units that barely communicated with their natural surroundings. But today's architecture must do much more: it not only needs to offer spaces for living and working but also make an active contribution to improving our environment and quality of life. In this context, "green architecture" is becoming more and more of a focus – a concept that integrates plants and green areas into the urban space and at the same time offers ecological, aesthetic, and social advantages.

The idea that plants make up an integral component of architecture is not a new one. Even ancient Rome turned to roof gardens and green courtyards to regulate the city climate and create a pleasant atmosphere. But only in the last decades has green architecture developed into a real trend, not only viewed as an aesthetic design element but primarily as an effective building block for sustainable and future-proof urban development. Buildings with greenery represent a crucial aspect of this transformation that is redefining the relationship between people, buildings, and nature. The projects presented in this book show the varied and imaginative ways in which architects, landscape architects, urban planners, and designers approach the topic of green building envelopes. Buildings blend in with nature, are overgrown with lush greenery, cultivate plant-covered grids, or become hard to even recognize as buildings at first glance.

One of the greatest benefits of green architecture is that it improves the urban microclimate. In many cities, the growing practice of sealing surfaces and loss of green spaces is leading to a dramatic temperature rise in the area, which is referred to as an "urban heat island". Heat builds up in places where concrete and asphalt dominate, which causes a considerable rise in the air temperature during the summer months. This effect not only comes with unpleasant consequences for city dwellers' well-being, but also increases energy needs to cool the buildings. Plants, on the other hand, boast a natural cooling ability. They absorb $CO^2$, release oxygen, and evaporate water, which can tangibly lower the ambient temperature. A green façade or roof can thereby act as a type of air-conditioning "green roof" that not only reduces the air temperature but also improves the air quality. Particularly in densely populated urban areas, where the air exchange is often limited, plants can make a significant contribution to reducing pollution and enhancing residents' well-being.

In addition to climatic advantages, green architecture offers significant benefits when it comes to quality of life. The connection between nature and architecture has a calming and restorative effect on people. In times when stress and a hectic pace often dominate everyday life, plants provide tranquility and regeneration. The view of green spaces, leaves rustling in the wind, buzzing bees and other insects – all of these elements contribute to biodiversity and to a positive, often therapeutic atmosphere. The feeling of living or working in a green

*Exterior view of the green-covered pyramidal extension of the Bunker St. Pauli in Hamburg.*

# Preface

environment considerably improves people's quality of life and well-being.
Green façades and roofs not only offer aesthetic advantages but also create new spaces for social interaction. Roof gardens, balconies, and façades with plants often serve as social hubs, as places of relaxation and community. In densely populated cities with limited space for traditional gardens, these green oases provide a valuable alternative. They act as green retreats where you can escape the urban hustle and bustle without having to leave the city.
Green architecture is more than just a passing fad. It is a necessity arising from the current challenges of climate change and urban development. Integrating plants into façades, rooftops, and building envelopes is a future-oriented response to cities' urgent problems, such as temperature rises and air pollution, and improves quality of life.
This book presents a global selection of skillfully designed green building envelopes that live up to their promises. With sensual or sculptural expressions, wild and colorful as the seasons change – the selected projects depict consistently good, lively, and high-quality design. Let these astonishing projects surprise you…

8

# Shiroiya Hotel

## GUNMA | JAPAN

**Architect: Sou Fujimoto Architects**
**Year: 2020**
**Area: new 610.86 m² and renovation 713.53 m²**
**Further participants:**
**Ishi Sekkei, Solso**
**Technical features:**
**Connection between city, architecture and nature, for sustainable urban development.**

Originally founded over 300 years ago as a traditional inn, the building was forced to pave the way for a revitalized cityscape after its closure. The converted four-story concrete construction turned into the Heritage Tower, while a new building, the Green Tower, was erected next to it. In the early stages of the design process, the building was radically gutted to create a gigantic courtyard that serves as the "city's living room". The open-plan space with solid concrete pillars and exposed beams features skylights that flood the room with daylight and forms a piazza that connects various areas, such as art, plants, and furniture. The design of the staircases leads to a vertically structured space that recreates the experience of moving through a city – with constantly changing perspectives. The adjacent building is surrounded by a curved green bank that elevates the site and extends the urban pathway. This bank symbolizes the connection between old and new, outside and inside, and the urban and architectural dimension. The construction of the Shiroiya Ryokan was part of a comprehensive initiative promoted by Maebashi City in collaboration with entrepreneur Hitoshi Tanaka and local artists. The concept of "mebuku", which refers to growth and renewal, forms the core of these efforts. The Shiroiya project unites city, architecture, and nature, thereby contributing to sustainable urban development.

SHIROIYA

10

Plants mainly used: trees, shrubs and local grasses.

*Main entrance from the street. View of the Shiroiya Hotel completely covered with vegetation. Foyer view. Interior view of one room. Staircases.*

*Exterior view of the green building. Interior view. Section. First floor plan.*

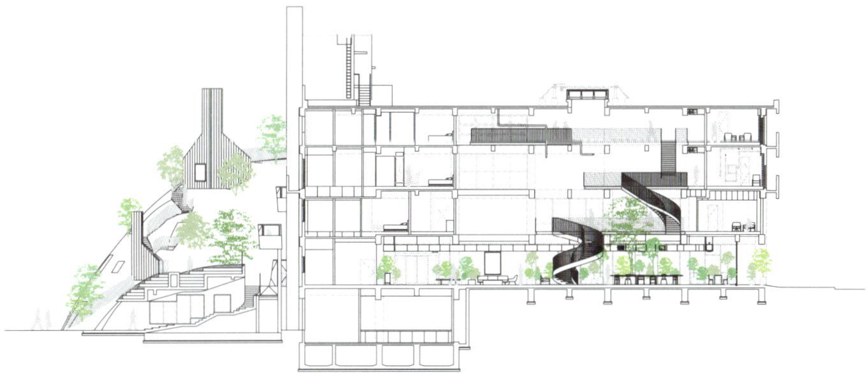

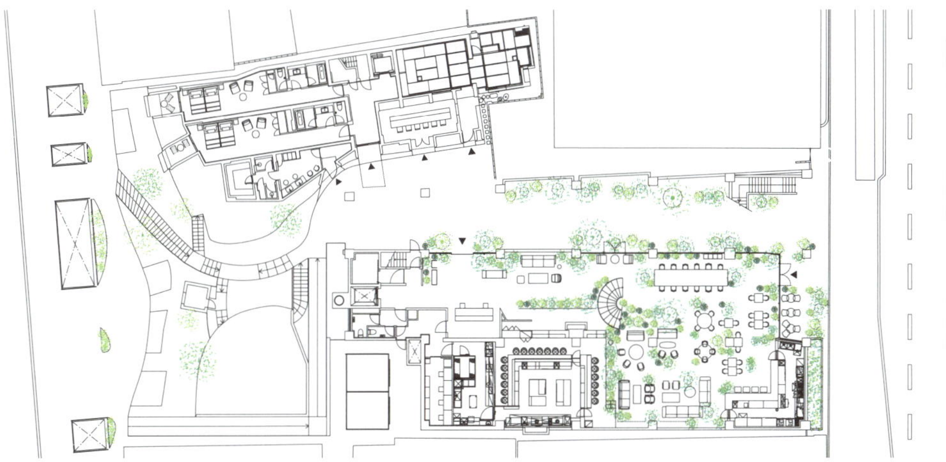

# Maggie's Yorkshire

## LEEDS | UNITED KINGDOM

**Architect: Heatherwick studio**
**Year: 2020**
**Area: 462 m$^2$**
**Further participants:**
**AKT II, Balston Agius, Blumer-Lehmann, Butler & Young, CDM Scotland, Gardiner & Theobald, Light Bureau, Max Fordham Consulting, Sir Robert McAlpine, Olsson Fire & Risk, Robert Lombardelli Partnership**
**Technical features:**
**Prefabricated spruce wood structure and breathable materials. Biophilic architecture.**

Situated on the St. James's University Hospital campus, Maggie's Centre in Leeds is the 26th center opened by the charity Maggie's in the UK, which offers free support to cancer patients. The building comprises three pavilion-like structures that encompass consultation rooms and shape the center with its open-plan kitchens and social areas such as a library and an exercise room. The architecture aligns with Maggie's philosophy that good design can promote healing. The sustainable wooden construction made of prefabricated spruce wood is complemented by breathable materials such as lime plaster, which regulates the room climate. A rooftop garden, designed by Balston Agius and inspired by the forests of Yorkshire, combines native plants with evergreen areas. Visitors are invited to help care for the more than 23,000 flower bulbs and 17,000 plants – a homage to Maggie Keswick Jenck's love for gardening. For the interior, the center resorts to natural materials, soft lighting, and varied rooms that allow for social interaction as well as silent retreat. Shelves and windowsills provide space for personal items, creating a sense of home. Maggie's Yorkshire has expanded Heatherwick studio's focus on biophilic architecture, as demonstrated by the EDEN residential tower in Singapore or the green 1000 Trees project in Shanghai. The center is open to cancer patients and their family and friends. Visitors receiving treatment at the hospital are also welcome.

14

*Main view of Maggie's Yorkshire. The center from the street. Interior view of a social area. Relaxation area. Floor plans. Interior view.*

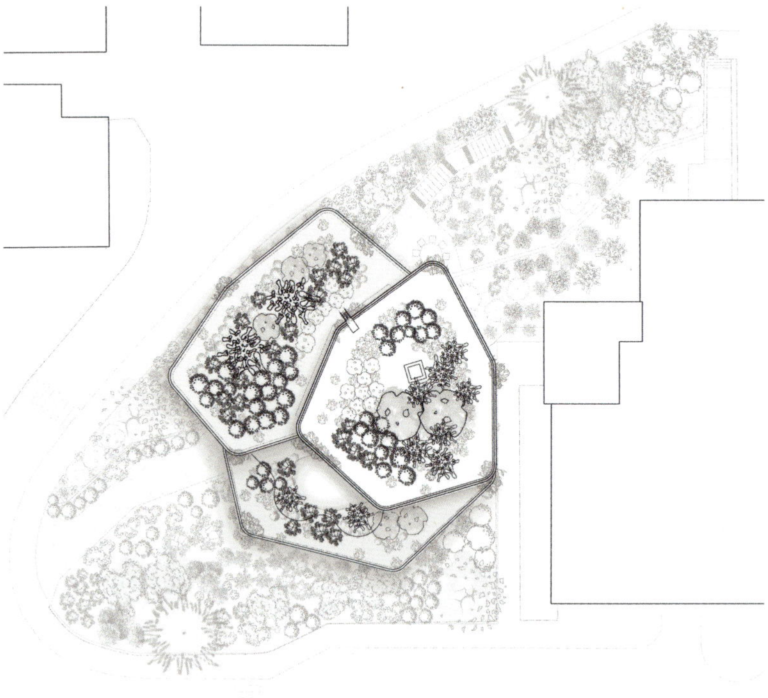

## Plants mainly used: 23,000 flower bulbs and 17,000 plants local to Yorkshire.

Herzlich Willkommen
Herzlich Willkommen

# Bunker St. Pauli

## HAMBURG | GERMANY

**Landscape Architect: Landschaftsarchitektur+ Holzapfel-Herziger & Benesch**
**Year: 2024**
**Area: 7,600 m² of green roof and 3,200 m² of vertical greening**
**Further participants: Mark Krieger, Ingrid Gock, Tree nursery Lorenz von Ehren**
**Technical features:**
**New structure on a protected historic monument. Green path uphill around the building with public rooftop garden. Cascading drainage system with retention boxes and intelligent flow restrictors.**

In the heart of Hamburg, the Bunker St. Pauli has turned into a striking new landmark. A 20-meter-tall pyramid-shaped extension, including plenty of greenery on the roof and façades, was added to the monumental historic structure from World War II. Initiated by residents and privately funded, the project aimed to open up access to the building's roof area to the public. Today, a 560-meter-long path takes visitors from the ground to the top, where a public roof garden offers a breathtaking panoramic view of the city. The building's new stories house a hotel, a restaurant, a music and sports hall, and host cultural events. In addition, a memorial site was set up beneath the new green roof. The landscape architecture designed by Hamburg's Landschaftsarchitektur+ studio demonstrates a detailed planting concept that includes evergreen shrubs, deciduous trees, and perennials. The design was devised with care to weather tricky locational conditions such as strong winds and the summer heat. The planting strategy envisages plants that intertwine and form a dense barrier that shields against the wind. Water management was another priority, with high substrate layers and restraint systems for collecting and storing precipitation on the roof. Excess water is stored in an underground cistern and reused for irrigation. A multi-year research project is currently examining how greenery impacts the building's energy management and the environment's microclimate. This project is a successful example of how climate adjustment measures can be integrated into historic buildings to create a harmonious combination of ecological, commercial, and social functions.

# 18

Number of species: more than 100. Plants mainly used: Pinus mugo, Amelanchier lamarckii, Acer campestre, Pinus sylvestris "Watereri".

*Main view from the street. View of the top level with public rooftop garden. Part of the 560-meter path leading to the top of the bunker. Roof plan. Side view.*

*View of the pyramid-shaped addition with green façade. The bunker with a 360-degree panoramic view of the city.*

20

# Villa M

## PARIS | FRANCE

**Architect: Triptyque**
**Year: 2021**
**Area: 8,000 m²**
**Further participants:**
**Philippe Starck, Coloco**
**Technical features:**
**Façade designed as an exoskeleton, with a minimalist and light look, composed by prefabricated pieces as in a construction game.**

Villa M marked a significant milestone in the development of Triptyque, as the company is expanding to Paris. The project combines 15 years of research and experiments with the concept of "natural culture", which was created in Brazil. The central theme of Villa M revolves around the tension between a perfectly rational constructive grid and its randomness or contrast to an organic element. Designed as a dynamic system, the building consistently represents the interplay between nature and culture, with the two forces vying for dominance throughout the seasons. By integrating hanging micro-gardens, aligned precisely with ceiling-high glazing, it creates a flowing connection between public and private spaces and thereby ensures a seamless transition between indoor and outdoor spaces. Villa M, a multi-functional, health-oriented hotel, is an innovative project by the Pasteur Mutuality Group. The project embodies the new generation of hybrid buildings in densely populated city areas where multi-functionality meets sustainability. It represents an impressive and enriching addition to the urban landscape, seamlessly combining design, nature, and function.

# 22

Number of species: 94. Plants mainly used: herbal plants, fruit trees and medium to large sized perennial species.

*View from below. Exterior view of the green façade. Villa M from the street. City view from the green rooftop terrace. Interior view.*

*Main view of the building's façade. Detail view of the façade. Section.*

# The Prow at Expedia Group

## WASHINGTON | USA

**Architect: Aidlin Darling Design**
**Year: 2020**
**Area: 225.6 m$^2$ interior conditioned space and 123.1 m$^2$ exterior deck**
**Further participants:**
**KPFF, Surfacedesign, Hart Crowser, WSP**
**Technical features:**
**Biophilic strategy to improve the connection with the environment. Sloping stone walls as plateau edges and local materials.**

On the Expedia Group's 40-hectare-campus in Seattle, The Prow offers a biophilic retreat for the company's employees, providing a refuge that clears the mind and thus promotes innovation. Its architecture is a precise gesture within the landscape: in the campus masterplan, the landscape architect devised a sequence of cascading plateaus that lead from the company's office all the way down to Elliott Bay. The Prow adds a series of 240-meter-long slanted stone walls to this structure, seamlessly merging the building's walls with the edges of the plateaus. Local materials from the Pacific Northwest shape the architectural palette, which reinforces the connection with the environment. The walls are made of the same stone as the embankments along Elliott Bay, while the floors and ceilings consist of Douglas fir timber from the region. Black-varnished steel structures discreetly recede into the background. The plant-covered roof smoothly connects with the ground level on two sides and conceals the building within its surroundings. Canted towards the bay, it rises from the landscape. Emerging from the land with a vector-like form, the design references the high-velocity motion at the heart of Expedia Group's business. Below the 15-meter-wide overhang, a floating deck provides a place to relax. Two fully glazed walls frame the breathtaking panoramic views of the bay and Mount Rainier behind it.

Number of species: over 20. Plants mainly used: Koeleria macrantha, two Sedum mixes, Nyssa sylvatica, Prunus x yedoensis, Quercus garryana trees.

*View of the exterior green roof.*
*Outdoor space. Aerial view.*
*View of the building integrated in the naturalistic context.*
*Axonometric section.*

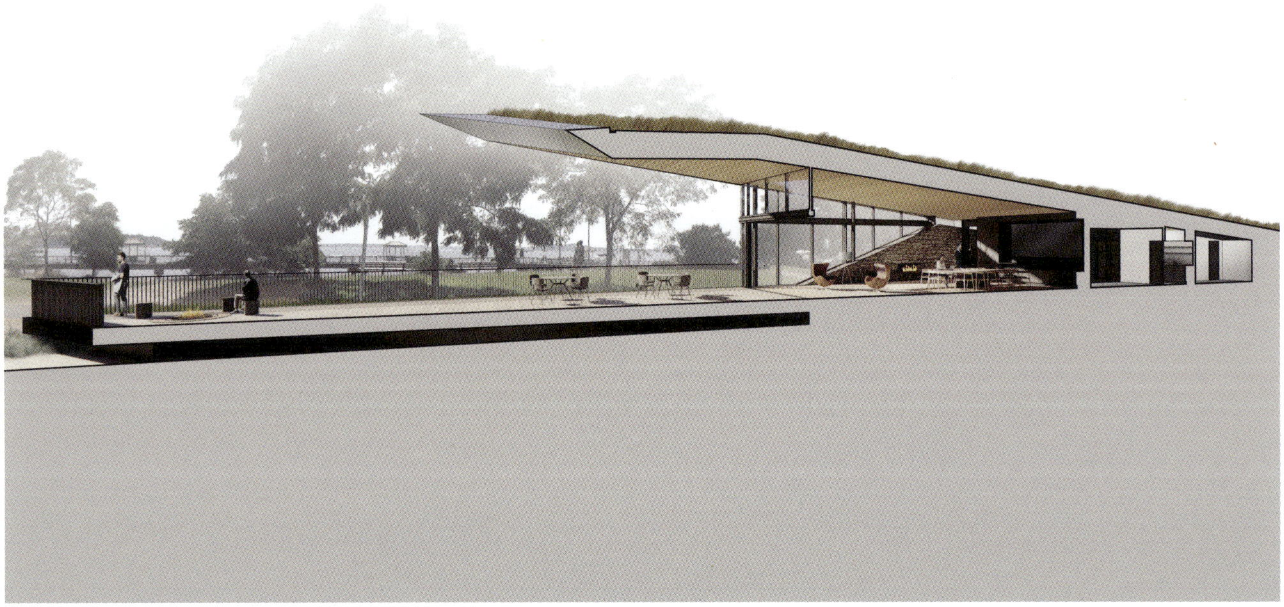

*Night view of the building.*
*Top view of the green roof integrated into the surrounding plateaus.*

# ASI Reisen Offices

## NATTERS | AUSTRIA

**Architect: Snøhetta**
**Year: 2019**
**Area: 1,389 m²**
**Further participants:**
**Tragwerkspartner zt and Alpsolar Klimadesign**
**Technical features:**
**Suspended metal façade construction as climbing scaffolding with accessible balcony areas.**

Snøhetta designed a new office with space for 65 employees for ASI Reisen, a travel provider offering individual and adventure trips. The concept for the wooden construction aimed to achieve symbiosis between nature and humanity – a topic that shapes ASI's work and was developed together with its employees. A "green curtain" helps the four-story building slot into its surroundings harmoniously. Inside, gallery rooms create a large, open, and flexible office space spanning several stories. A metal climbing frame hangs in front of the black wooden façade, also serving as a balcony on the west-facing side. The green façade, the appearance of which changes throughout the year, acts as a glare shield and provides shade for the expansive glass surfaces. The "green buffer zone" and its microclimate minimize the energy required to cool the building by around 18,000 kWh/year. The traditional yakisugi method was used to conserve timber. A thermal-dynamic building simulation supported the development of a sustainable energy concept. A reversible air-water heat pump system heats and cools the building. Room-temperature, humidity and $CO^2$ sensors control the natural ventilation, which makes use of thermal buoyancy and wind pressure. A photovoltaic system on the roof serves as a surplus system. The generated electricity covers part of the building's power consumption.

## Number of species: 17. Plants mainly used: Lonicera henryi, Lonicera caprifolium, Clematis montana, Aristolochia macrophylla, Parthenocissus tricuspidata "Veitchii".

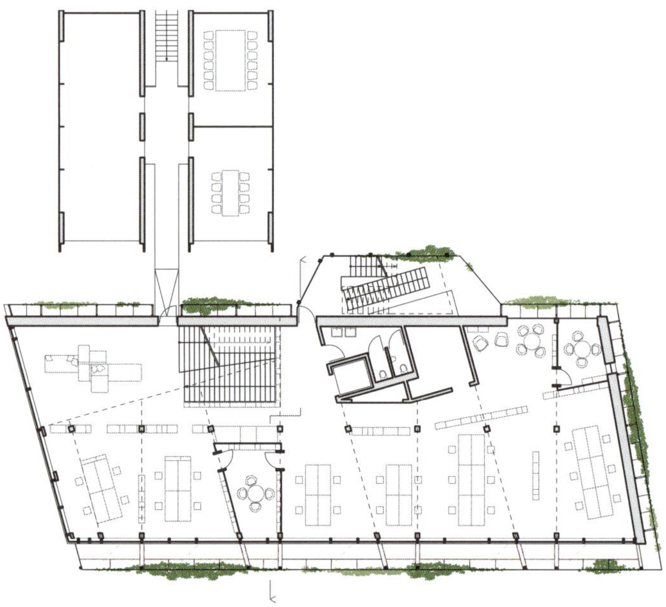

*Exterior view of the green façade. View of the common area. Metal façade with climbing plants. Interior view. Floor plan. Section. View of the building surrounded by the garden.*

32

# Tony Fruit Office

## HO CHI MINH CITY | VIETNAM

**Architect: TAA Design**
**Year: 2020**
**Area: 225 m²**
**Technical features:**
**Vegetation and perforated wooden frame as protection against overheating.**

Tony Fruit Office is located in Ho Chi Minh City's District 4, which features a high density of commercial hubs and office headquarters. From dawn to dusk, the sun shines directly on two of the building's main façades. This causes major problems of overheating in the interior. A perforated geometry creates an intermediate space that provides shade and establishes far-reaching visual contact between the building's interior and the urban environment. Setting back the hard construction also creates space for outdoor greenery, which produces a natural skin that covers the daylight-exposed façades. Protected by a blanket of plants, every office enjoys a fresh view of the greenery. Every level contains a system of similar green areas, with mutual visual contact from different floors. This ensures a pleasant atmosphere in each room. Wooden slats form cubes that provide effective shading from the daylight entering the building diagonally. At the same time, the reset glazing receives so much reflected light that it reduces the costs of cooling and lighting in building maintenance. Perforated with greenery, the block offers a potential solution to improving the working conditions in buildings in cities with a tropical environment.

TÓNY
FRUIT
OFFICE

## Plants mainly used: trees, shrubs and cascading plants.

*View from below. Tony Fruit Office from the street. Green façade. Aerial view of the building. View from a green-covered balcony.*

*View from above of Tony Fruit Office covered with vegetation. Top view. Axonometric view.*

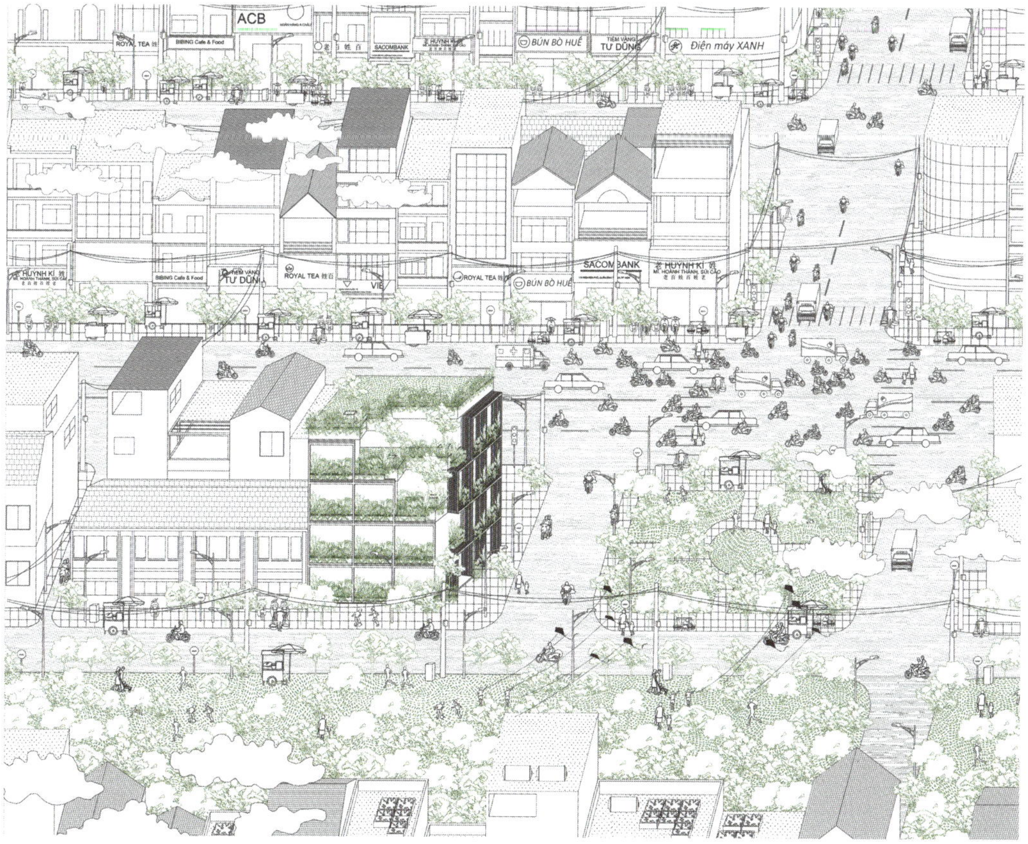

36

# Library in the Earth

## CHIBA | JAPAN

**Architect: Hiroshi Nakamura & NAP**
**Year: 2022**
**Area: 113.09 m²**
**Further participants:**
**Kanebako Structural Engineers, SUMITOMO FORESTRY, SOLSO**
**Technical features:**
**Reinforced roof with a "mutual aid structure" in the reading room. Circular skylight created by overlapping vertical beams.**

Library in the Earth is a retreat for people who spend sunny days on the field and rainy days with books. Situated on Kurkku Fields, an agricultural production site, it follows the principle of designing architecture as part of nature instead of interfering with it. The structure sits in a depression that was once filled with rubble. The goal was to return the valley to its lush original state – a tribute to the "mother pond", which is hugely significant to the farmers. The library is shaped like a sliver in the earth, which looks like a drop of water from an aerial view. Visitors can access a corridor of bookshelves by passing through plowed ground. The project avoided traditional architectural elements such as columns and beams: Instead, concrete slabs overhang supporting walls, while walls, floors, and ceilings are seamlessly connected with the clay coating. At the edge of the structure, the grass grows to the border and drapes down like a living curtain – a detail that stores moisture and regulates irrigation in line with the season. The interior rooms follow the natural topography: they feature low ceilings, hidden nooks for children, and a storytelling room at the rear. In this honeycomb-like retreat, folded bookshelves surround the tiered seating areas. Their narrow, vertical frames carry each other in a circular structure that only remains stable through the principle of mutual support. At the highest point, a skylight opening frames a view of the sky and clouds – a poetic allusion to the close connection between agriculture, nature, and community. This library contemplates the earth – by literally hiding within it and preserving its wisdom.

Number of species: 35. Plants mainly used: Zoysia japonica.

*Exterior view of the Library in the Earth. Exterior of the front garden. Interior view of the library. Longitudinal section.*

*Exterior view of the building completely covered by vegetation. Interior of the library with large window to the garden.*

# Urban Forest

## BRISBANE | AUSTRALIA

**Architect: Koichi Takada Architects**
**Year: planned for 2028**
**Area: 47,000 m²**
**Further participants:**
**Developer - Aria Property Group**
**Technical features:**
**Principles of passive design. Solar panels. Vegetation as natural solar insulation. Rainwater and graywater irrigation.**

Urban Forest is a high-rise residential building with a deep connection to nature, situated in South Brisbane, a culturally rich district of Brisbane, Australia. Featuring a green, living façade with more than 27,000 plants, the project embodies the goal of bringing nature back into the cities. Instead of working with hard, industrial materials like concrete, steel, and glass, architect Koichi Takada chose to create a living architecture. In light of the global attention that the 2032 Olympic Games will bring to Brisbane, the goal of Urban Forest is to construct an iconic, sustainable building with 382 apartments. Tall, trunk-like pillars arise from the ground and create a publicly accessible green area on the 2,784-square-meter property. On the roof, two stories of the community facilities provide a place that promotes social interactions among residents and supports social sustainability. Passive design principles make optimal use of the subtropical climate, maximize daylight, and allow for natural ventilation. The vegetation is irrigated with rain and gray water and offers solar isolation, while solar panels generate renewable energy. The plants for the façade are cultivated outside of the property and will cover an area three times the size of the grounds once they are installed.

Number of species: 251. Plants mainly used: Tuckeroo, Lily pilly, Wisteria, Dwarf banksia, Coastal rosemary, Kangaroo fern, Native frangipani, Queensland monstera.

*Exterior view of the façade from below. Interior view of one apartment. Rooftop view at sunset. One terrace surrounded by plants. Main view of the building.*

*Entrance of the building completely surrounded by greenery. Green rooftop view at night.*

# Tainan Market

## TAINAN | TAIWAN

Architect: MVRDV
Year: 2022
Area: 12,331 m²
**Further participants:**
**LLJ Architects, The Urbanists Collaborative, Columbus Engineering Consultants**
**Technical features:**
**Wholesale vegetable and fruit market under green farming roof.**

The open-air Tainan Market not only serves as an important hub for Tainan's food supply chain but also as a meeting place and spot for social gatherings. The building's accessible roof offers a fantastic view of the surrounding landscape, which promotes tourism in the region. The building designed by MVRDV reinterprets the wholesale market by combining it with a public green space. The accessible rooftop consists of gently curved hills and terraces that are adorned with lively plants and reveal a vista of the surroundings. The structure's open-plan design allows for natural ventilation, ensuring comfort even on the hottest of Taiwan's summer days. While it currently accommodates a park, the roof could also be transformed into an educational farm that teaches children how to grow food and how the supply chain works. The market in Tainan is situated in a convenient location between the city and the mountains and combines functionality with aesthetics. It reflects the region's natural beauty and is suitable for both distributors and visitors.

Number of species: 22. Plants mainly used: fruit trees and herbs. New plants can be introduced following roof farming operation.

*View from above. The roof covered with vegetation. Interior view of the market. Aerial view. Building on the green roof. Green rooftop.*

*Front view of the Tainan Market.*
*Elevation. Roof plan.*

ul. I. Krasickiego
20/22
Wierzbno

# Foundation for Polish Science Headquarters

## WARSAW | POLAND

**Architect: FAAB Architektura**
**Year: 2014**
**Area: 2,180 m²**
**Further participants:**
**Semper Green Vertical Systems**
**Technical features:**
**Panels applied on the existing building/ renovation. Custom irrigation system supplied with rain water.**

The project aimed to preserve the character of an apartment building constructed in 1933 and heavily damaged during World War II, while also transforming it into a modern, environmentally friendly office building. Efforts were made to protect valuable architectural and historical elements, and particular attention was paid to compliance with the strict provisions of Warsaw's preservation order on construction volume and window arrangement. The location in a loosely built-up settlement from the 1930's influenced the building's multi-layered integration into the green surroundings and the public space. The goal was to minimize the impact on the urban infrastructure and the environment. By forgoing any fencing, the plot expands the public road space and visually ties in the rear garden with its surroundings. An atrium and openings on the ground floor, starting at the main entrance, establish a link between the interior and exterior space and between the road and the garden. A vertical garden installed on the façade – the first of its kind in the region – strengthens the building's connection with its green surroundings. Collected rainwater from a water-retaining structure irrigates the garden and reduces the need for municipal water. In total, 82% of the property is water-permeable, including the vertical garden. 96% of the aboveground surfaces and 100% of the underground parking area, receive daylight. The historic staircase with green terrazzo steps and rare, colorful ceramic tiles was preserved and reflects the atmosphere of European buildings from this era.

*Exterior view of the renovated building. View of the building covered with plants. Detail of the green façade.*

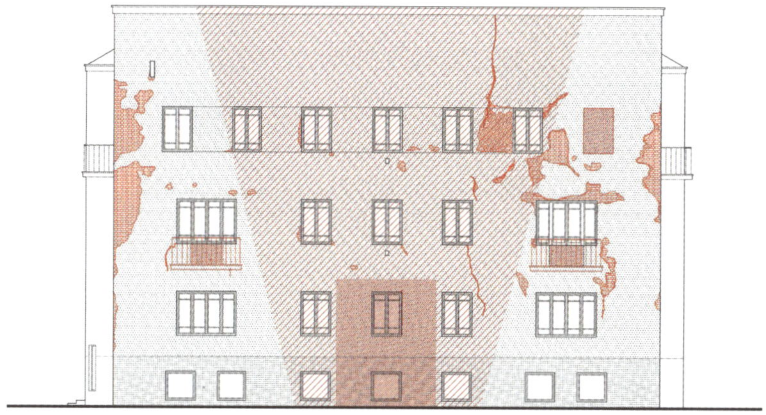

*Main exterior view of the building. Elevation before the renovation work.*

## Number of species: 20. Plants mainly used: Physocarpusopulifolus, Bergenia cordifolia, Hosta hybride, Waldsteinia ternata, Ligustrum sinense, Lonicera nitida.

# Office for Trees

## KHANH HOA | VIETNAM

**Architect: Pham Huu Son Architects**
**Year: 2024**
**Area: 650 m²**
**Further participants:**
**NHA XANH 79 Company**
**Technical features:**
**Solar panels. Rainwater harvesting systems. Use of fish waste to fertilize plants.**

Sustainable architecture in harmony with nature: with this concept in mind, the project connects the two main areas of the building. These spaces – a flexible work and reception room and a model house – offer customers an immersive spatial and interior experience. A large mango tree at the center of the property remained in place and forms the heart of a garden that separates the office unit and the model house. An underground water tank with 30 cubic meters capacity collects rainwater, which is then fed into the fishpond. Once filtered, it irrigates the roof's greenery and the surrounding garden via an automated pump system – a closed water circuit that saves resources. Planters on the roof cool the interior space, while ventilation slits and large glass surfaces eliminate the need for air-conditioning. The targeted arrangement of the greenery helps maximize the daylight. In addition, solar panels supply the entire office with renewable energy. The building was constructed with unfired bricks – a sustainable, locally available material. In combination with the use of rainwater, natural lighting, and photovoltaics, the Office for Trees by Pham Huu Son Architects sets an example for future-oriented, ecological architecture.

Number of species: 120. Plants mainly used: Bird of paradise, Bamboo, Jasmine plant, Porcelain flower, Licuala grandis palm.

*Exterior view from the garden. Interior view. Dining area open to the garden. Main entrance. Interior view of the living area.*

*Top view of the green roof.*
*Longitudinal section.*
*First floor plan. Roof plan.*

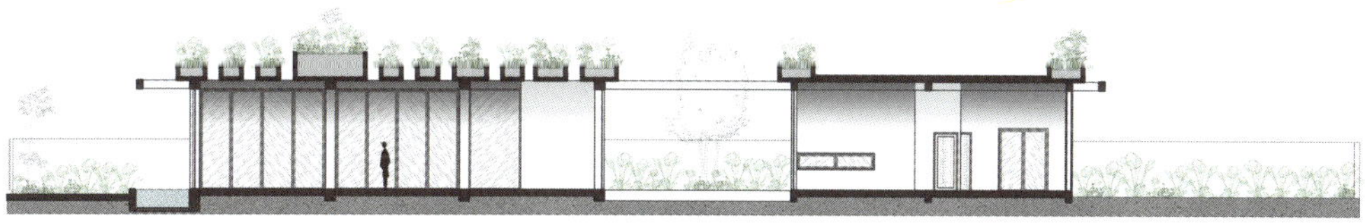

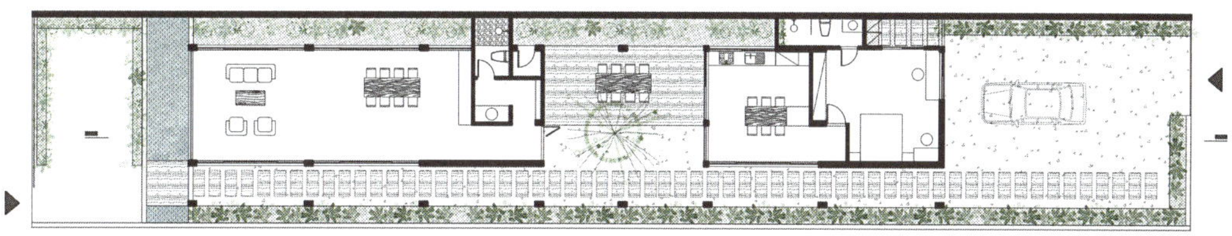

# FENDI Factory

## FLORENCE | ITALY

**Architect: Piuarch**
**with Antonio Perazzi**
**Year: 2022**
**Area: 14,000 m$^2$**
**Further participants:**
**MarsigliLab**
**Technical features:**
**Continuous and expansive green roof as an integrated ecological system.**

An elevated garden aimed to balance out a longstanding rift in the terrain and the slope on which it lies. This is the new FENDI Factory in Bagno a Ripoli (Florence). A complex spanning about 14,000 square meters, towering above the Tuscan landscape, designed to meet the high landscape design and progressive energy efficiency standards, an architectural landmark of exceptionally aesthetic and ecological value. Piuarch designed a building that stretches horizontally across a single level to create a free form, driven by the demands of the production process. This turns the rooms' practicability into the conceptual principle of the layout, which combines different functions and brings them together through fluid paths that cross the building horizontally. The complex comprises administrative offices, a production warehouse, manufacturing areas, a cafeteria, workshops, and a school for high-quality leather goods. The building, which almost appears to be subterranean due to the decision to establish a continuous and expansive green roof, becomes an integrated ecological system that emulates the contours of the land and recreates the shape of the original hill. A vast roof garden that takes on not only an ecological but also a social and community role and serves as a user-friendly room as well as a meeting place for employees. Seven hectares of greenery surround the factory, a perfect mixture of forests and agricultural landscapes in rural Tuscany.

FENDI

Number of species: 98. Plants mainly used: park / olive grove of 650 plants, mix of herbaceous and evergreen plants. Each court / mediterranean scrub tree species.

*View of a courtyard. Main exterior view of FENDI Factory. The green roof as a continuation of the surrounding vegetation. Exterior view. Interior view.*

*The production area opens up to the outside with a large glass façade for a high quality workplace. Axonometries. Design concept.*

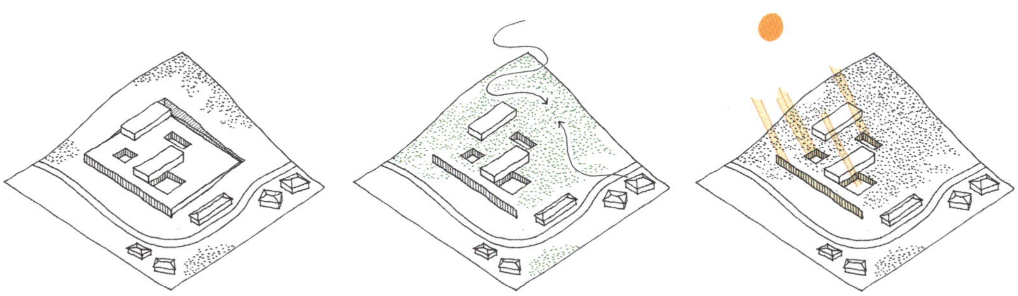

# Dune House

## MASSACHUSETTS | USA

Architect: Studio Vural
Year: 2019
Area: 320 m²
Design Team:
Selim Vural, Sumeyye Ozturk and Angela Tasveska
Technical features:
Concrete shell burrowed in sand dune and supported by concrete piles.

Dune House is an off-the-grid beach house designed for the coast of Cape Cod, MA. Thanks to geothermal and solar-energy systems, the house is completely self-sufficient. The ancient construction technique of burrowing, which uses the earth as an insulator, helps maximize efficiency. Even though Dune House is partially underground, its main living areas are spacious and bright. They offer wonderful views of the ocean and the beautiful scenery that surrounds the building. Dune House was designed as a prototype for the future of single-family homes.

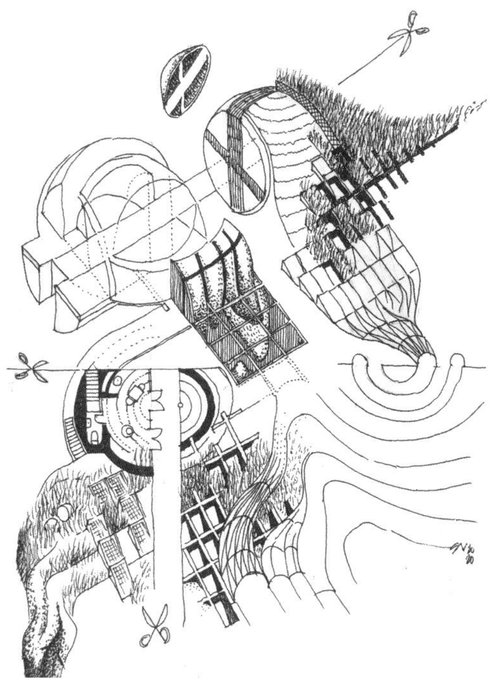

## Number of species: estimated 35. Plants mainly used: local grasses and shrubs.

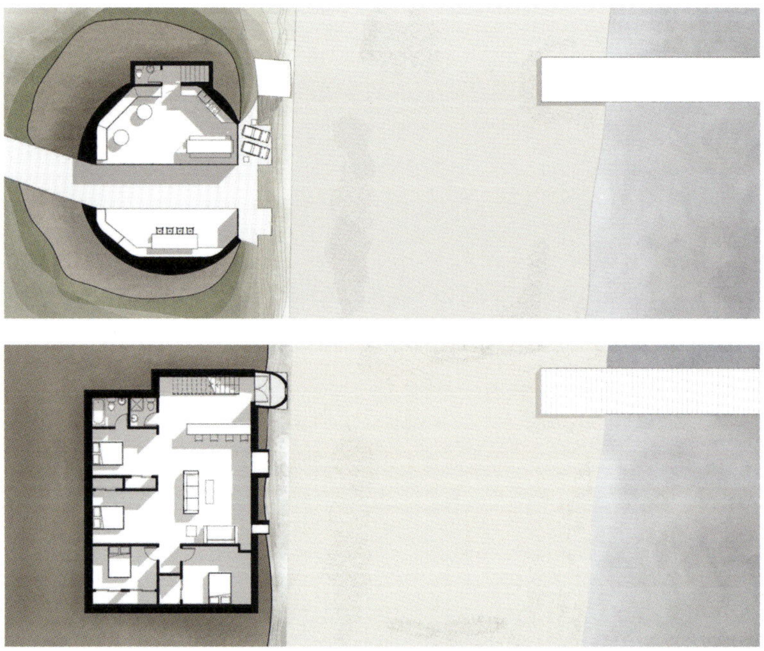

*Exterior view of the green-covered Dune House. Interior view of the living room. Sketch. Exterior view from the surrounding nature. Floor plans. Interior view.*

*Main view of Dune House from the water. Night view.*

# OLA HALE Restaurant and Bar

## HO CHI MINH CITY | VIETNAM

**Architect: CHIO Architects (Singapore)**
**Year: 2023**
**Area: 688 m²**
**Further participants:**
**CHIO Architects Landscape and BARIS Arch**
**Technical features:**
**Adaptive Reuse Project.**

OLA HALE Restaurant and Bar serves as an example of adaptive reuse and unites a single-story shop and a three-story residential building on the corner of Hai Ba Trung Road in Ho Chi Minh City, Vietnam. Featuring a striking Hawaiian theme, it complements the iconic Tan Dinh church on the opposite side. One of the design's crucial characteristics was a courtyard in front of the cafe, surrounded by a wall made of round perforated bricks and exposed concrete. This wall opens towards the church, steers the entrance in this direction, and invites passers-by to leave the bustling street and venture into the lush courtyard. Inside, a unique design awaits visitors. Ceilings of turquoise linen represent the motion of the Hawaiian waters through various details – ebbs, tides, and waves. They alternate in line with the area's function: cafe, restaurant, or bar. The design captures the energy and beauty of the ocean and creates a dynamic atmosphere. It includes specific viewpoints, such as a frameless glass window on the second floor of the restaurant, while the third floor and the roof terrace offer vast panoramas of the Tan Dinh church. To counter the lack of green space in the area, façades with plants were integrated. These are attached to lamellae with a wooden look, preserving the building's original style. The project shows the potential of adaptive reuse in Ho Chi Minh City, combines green strategies, and preserves the charm of existing structures. The building is considered pioneering in the transformation of Hai Ba Trung Road.

Number of species: 14. Plants mainly used:
Sword ferns, Foxtail grass, Hibiscus, Frangipani,
Curtain creeper philodendron, Bird of paradise.

*Main view of the building. Interior view of the restaurant. Exterior façade with greenery and large windows. View from below. Terrace with view.*

*Outdoor area surrounded by plants. Detail of the bathroom open to the green. First and second floor plans.*

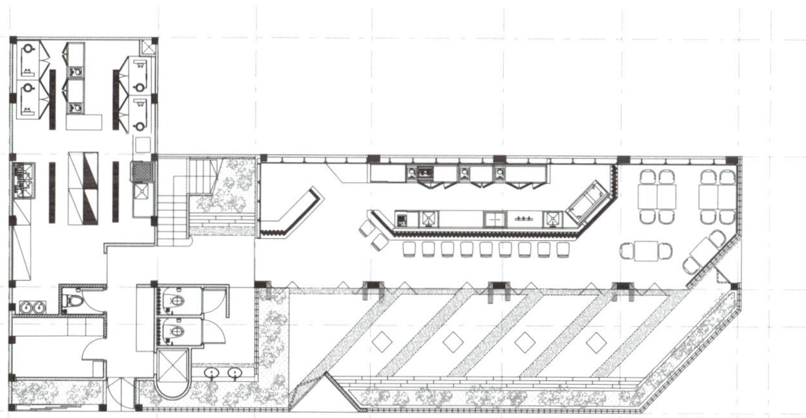

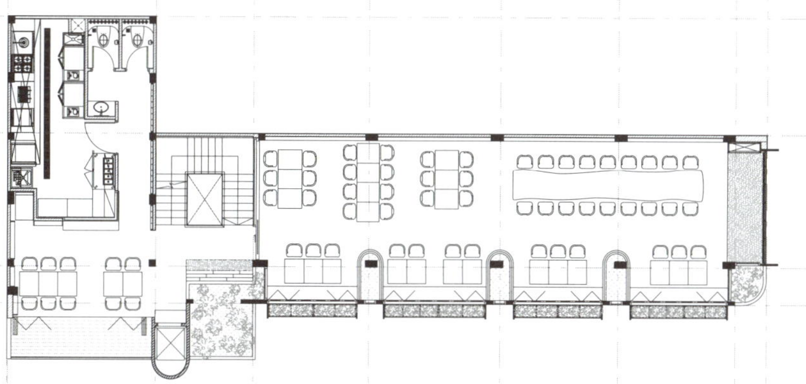

# Casa Abacateiro

## FLORIANÓPOLIS | BRASIL

**Architect: Ana Ruivo, Baixo Impacto Arquitetura**
**Year: 2022**
**Area: 275 m$^2$**
**Further participants:**
**daTerra Construções, Monte Sião Paisagismo**
**Technical features:**
**Raw earth walls. Reclaimed wood structure. Green roofs. Bioclimatic design. Natural hand made paint.**

Casa Abacateiro was designed with the aim of creating a spacious, inviting home that seamlessly blurs the boundaries between inside and outside. The architecture is divided into two areas. The southwest block comprises the bedrooms, bathrooms, and the service area, whereas the northeast block with recycled wood and metal carriers offers open-plan rooms and wide openings to the outdoor area. The green roofs are a bioclimatic highlight, controlling the natural ventilation and lighting. In the summer, they provide shade, and in the winter, they let in sunlight through openings and transparent bamboo surfaces. Tall openings support cooling through the chimney effect. The rooftop gardens increase thermal inertia and reduce the heat island effect, while also offering an attractive path to the highest point of the house and opening up to a view of the ocean. Between the two blocks sits a large wall made of raw earth, constructed with the artisanal and traditional "wattle and daub" technique. During the day, it retains the warmth of the winter sun. It then gradually releases this warmth, thereby regulating the humidity. Durable, ecological, and sustainable materials such as wood and natural lime plaster were used to complete the project. The aesthetic focuses on the materials' raw texture and their harmonious interconnection.

## Number of species: 15. Plants mainly used: Peumus boldus, Strelitzia reginae, Aerva sanguinolenta (L.), Tradescantia pallida Commelinaceae.

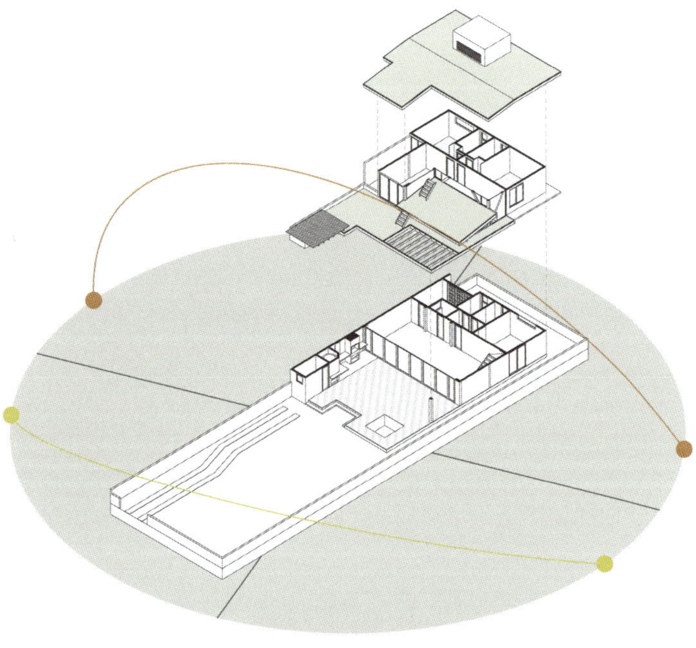

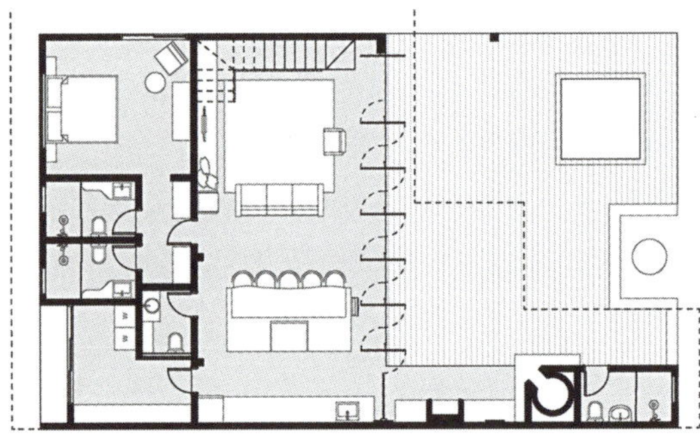

*Exterior view of the roof and green terrace. Interior view. Exterior view of the house. Living room open to the outdoor terrace. Axonometrie. Floor plan. Exterior view.*

72

# Jipyoung Guesthouse

## GYEONGSANGNAM-DO | KORFA

**Architect: Byoung Cho / BCHO Partners**
**Year: 2018**
**Area: 3,270 m²**
**Further participants:**
**Kim Yong Taek, Landscape Design Studio KnL**
**Technical features:**
**Reinforced concrete volumes embedded in the ground and blended into the landscape.**

Burrowing into the earth, sinking down, blending into the horizon – Jipyoung Guesthouse on Korea's southern coast celebrates architecture that meets the forces of nature with humility. The name "Jipyoung", which translates to "horizon earth", reflects this concept: the house opens up towards the sky, while a large portion of its mass is embedded into the cliff. Instead of asserting itself against the ocean and the wind, it allows nature to embrace it and gently slots into the landscape. While coastal construction is displacing the natural environment, this project engages in a dialog with it. The building is cut into the hillside, so the view from inside looks directly out on the ocean – so visitors wake up amidst the vibrancy of nature. Surrounded by a defiant topography and a winding road, the building is anchored deep in the fold of the ground, a gesture of returning to the earth. Jipyoung is more than a holiday home. It is a place of reflection that welcomes guests from all over Korea. Here, architecture and landscape fuse into an experiential space that offers tranquility and raises awareness of nature's fragile beauty. In the symbiosis between constructed and naturally grown world, a deep harmony reveals itself – a retreat that makes the essence of the earth tangible.

Number of species: 20. Plants mainly used: Acer palmatum, Miscanthus sinensis, Spiraea japonica, Veronica linariaefolia, Epilobium pyrricholophum.

*View from above. The grassed roof embedded in the surrounding nature. One bedroom. Top view of the Jipyoung Guesthouse. Floor plans.*

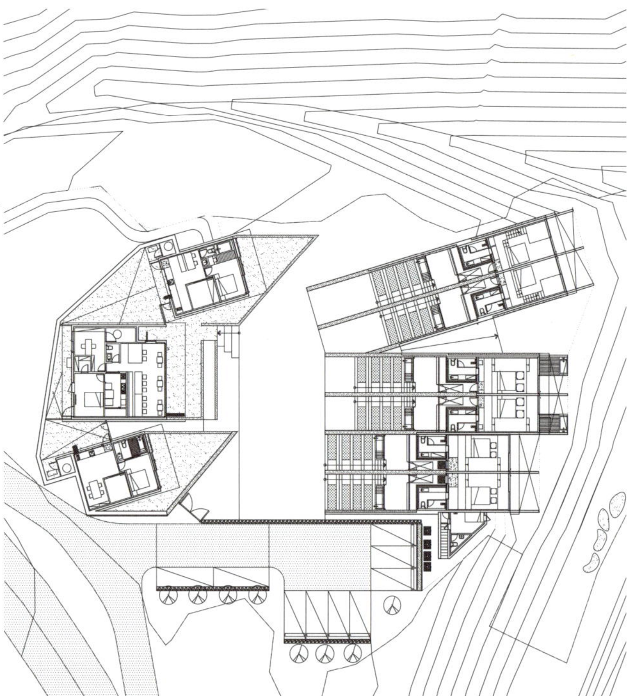

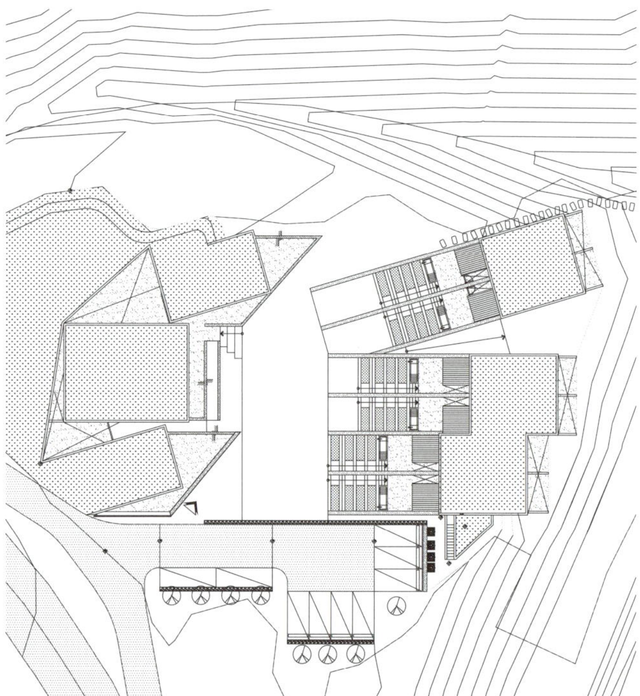

*Front view of the building and the green roof. Detail of the concrete cafeteria dining table.*

# Green Field Factory of Karupannya

## RANGPUR | BANGLADESH

**Architect: Nakshabid Architects**
**Year: 2016**
**Area: 14,170 m²**
**Further participants:**
**Saidul Huq Juice Landscape and Interior**
**Technical features:**
**Green screen. Light-well. Water reservoir.**

The Green Field Factory operated by Karupannya Rangpur Limited offers an example of sustainable architecture and socially responsible design. One of the project's key goals was to create a workspace that could serve as a place to relax and be close to nature. The design of the factory in Robertsongoni, Rangpur, Bangladesh, revolved around the climate situation and aimed to maximize energy efficiency and comfort. Forgoing air conditioning, the building's intelligent design ensures pleasant temperatures: plant-covered façades, water surfaces, and atria facilitate natural cooling and ventilation. Daylight penetrates the interior rooms, while vertical gardens improve the air quality. The seven-story main building, consisting of concrete and exposed brickwork, is both functional and aesthetic. In addition to the workspaces, it features a front garden, a Nandini park on the daycare center's roof, and countless sculptures that enliven the space. The design strengthens the connection between humanity and nature. Women – who make up 80% of the workforce – enjoy a sense of security and independence here. This sustainable architecture has received multiple awards, including the "UIA 2030 Award" and "RIBA International Award for Excellence".

## Plants mainly used: native plants.

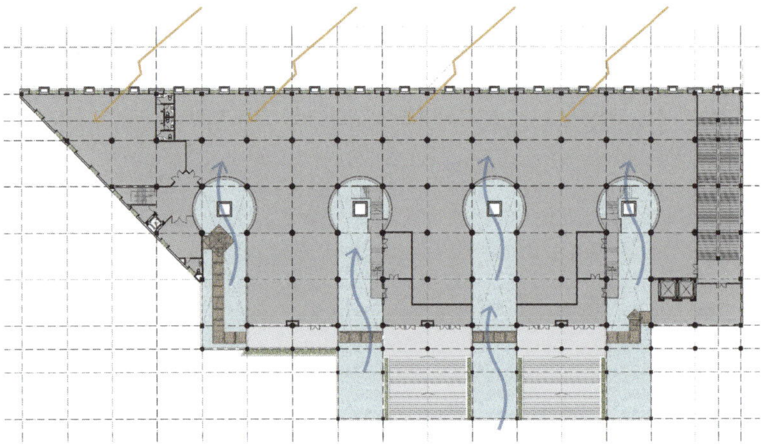

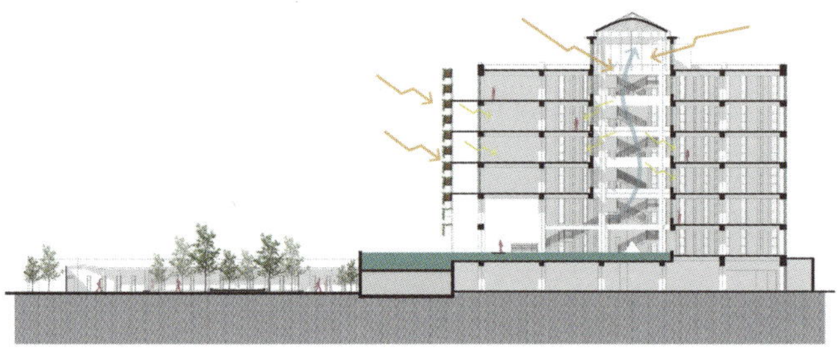

*View of the entrance with green façade. Interior view. Aerial view. Detail of the pond. Floor plan. Section. View of the green building overlooking the garden.*

# Grüner Pavillon

## ST. GALLEN | SWITZERLAND

**Architect: Tom Munz Architekt*innen**
**Year: 2020**
**Area: 152 m²**
**Further participants:**
**Kollektiv Nordost, Borgogno Eggenberger Partner AG, Studer und Strauss**
**Technical features:**
**Timber construction with climbing plants and bindweed. Natural irrigation.**

The Grüne Pavillon – green pavilion – is situated in St. Gallen's botanical garden and serves many different purposes: as a training room, lecture hall, foyer, event location, office, and storage space. The botany – as a reference to the location and a thematic anchor point – drapes the fully glazed structure in green plant life. A wooden supporting structure forms the pavilion's framework. Bindweed and climbing plants rise up along wire ropes around the pavilion and provide visual protection and shade in the summer. On the roof, a specially designed natural-rubber seal and a thick layer of soil retains rainwater for a long time. This provides natural irrigation for the native orchids in an optimal cycle of water and humidity, while the excess water flows into the surrounding plots. Inside, a cube of built-in wardrobes divides the open space into an entry space, main room, and storage space. The building benefits from natural climate control. The ceiling-high, barred ventilation flaps provide diagonal ventilation and cooling. Together with the green façade, this ensures heat protection in the summer without active cooling. The pavilion's wooden frame consists of regional spruce wood. The floor is made of a sealed and polished concrete slab. Concrete and wood absorb and store the sun's heat, slowly releasing it during the night.

## Number of species: 21. Plants mainly used: Bryonia alba and vine plants.

*Exterior view of the pavilion covered with vegetation. Interior view. Grüner Pavillon façade. View from the garden. Side view.*

Wood and glass façade with climbing plants. Interior view. Floor plan. Long section.

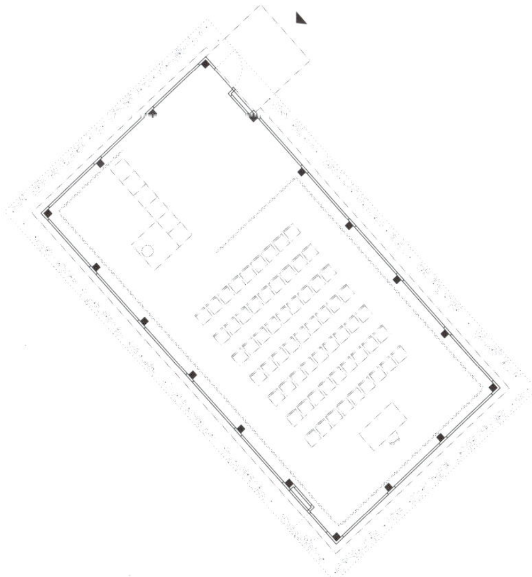

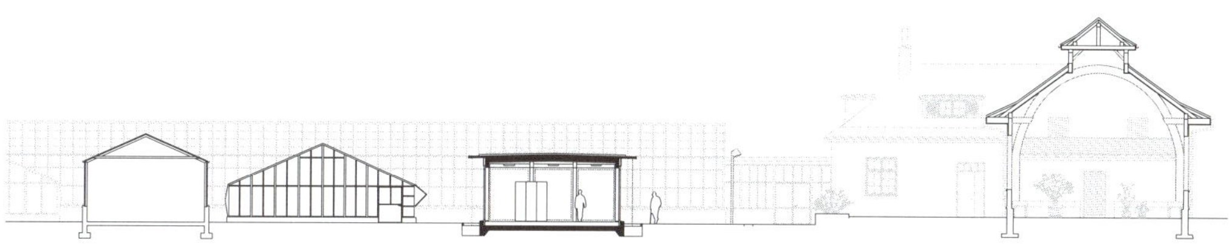

# Hôtel De Ville Herstal

## HERSTAL | BELGIUM

**Architect: AAFH!**
**Year: 2015**
**Area: 12,500 m²**
**Further participants: Louis Benech Paris**
**Technical features: Individual green wall tiles with their water supply.**

The new city administration of Herstal, Belgium, is setting new standards in urban design with its innovative green façade. Instead of a monolithic slab of greenery, a chessboard pattern of plant modules, glass, and solid panels adorns the 2,500-square-meter outer shell – around 1,000 square meters of which is covered with vegetation. In contrast to traditional green façades, the individual plant elements are autonomous. Every square can be replaced individually, which not only ensures easy care and maintenance, but also allows for a large variety of plants. 23,000 plants were used in total, selected by water storage capacity, insulating effect, and the respective module's orientation towards the sun. For advice on the botanical design, the architects turned to Louis Benech, the renowned landscape architect who renovated the Tuileries Garden in Paris. Every green module has its own water supply at the top, creating a closed irrigation circuit. In addition to their aesthetic effect, the plants contribute to the building's energy efficiency: they have a cooling effect in the summer and an insulating effect in the winter – as is typical for green roofs. In this way, Herstal Hôtel De Ville combines sustainability with innovative design and creates architecture that breathes, grows, and interacts with the city.

The façade from below. Exterior view of the building. Main view from the street. View of the façade. Floor plan. Axonometrie.

Number of species: 23,000. Plants mainly used: Splenium scolopendrium, Ajuga reptans, Armeria maritima, Campanula, Carex, Epimedium.

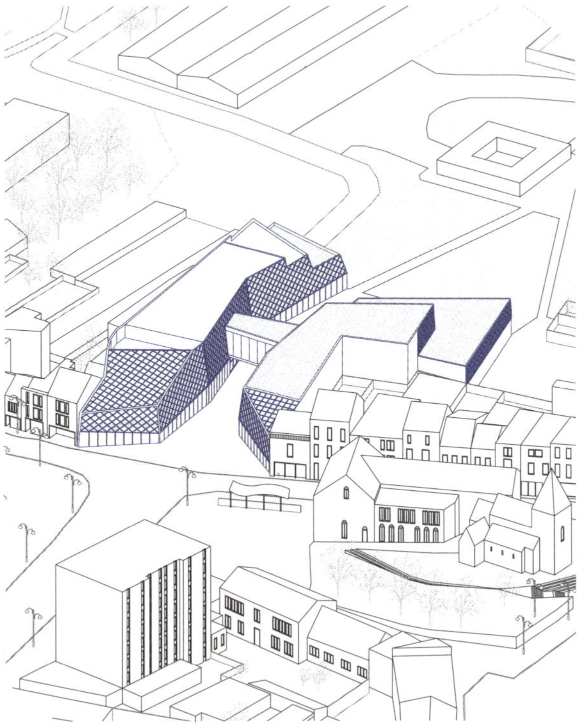

*View of the main entrance. Exterior façade covered with panels, glass and vegetation.*

88

# MIA Design Studio Office

## HO CHI MINH CITY | VIETNAM

**Architect: MIA Design Studio**
**Year: 2020**
**Area: 410 m²**
**Technical features:**
**Structure with reinforced concrete frame and slab system. Floor finished by polishing the original reinforced concrete slab. Exterior walls built with plastered brick and finished with water-based paint.**

Large desks for architects and a vertical library form the focal point of the project. 360-degree window openings reveal a view of the greenery, while the tropical light is filtered in a targeted way at 60 centimeters above the tables. Overhanging windowsills add to this, not only serving as sun protection, but also doubling the size of the work surfaces. The upper window areas can be used as pinboards for sketches, pictures, and notes – where inspiration and functionality intersect. Behind every workspace sits an open library with carefully selected material samples and models. These are integrated organically into a central structure that serves as a vertical staircase and also creates a dynamic space composition. While the work zones unfold vertically, the ground floor acts as an open-plan communication space. This is where contemporary climate concepts of Vietnamese architecture are tested: a glass border connects the "field of ideas" – a minimalist garden made of boulders – with the interior room. This interim space, the "gray zone", acts as an intersection between structure and emptiness, light and shade, function and atmosphere. In architecture, gray equates to an infinite scale between the constants of black and white – space for change and individuality. Here, minimalism becomes a lesson: the true value lies in reduction. The connection between time and space results in moods that change throughout the day. Light and shadow, the way the leaves blow in the wind, chirping birds – all of this shapes an environment that feels alive. A studio that is not just a place of work, but also a home for ideas.

Number of species: 3. Plants mainly used:
Vernonia elliptica, Bamboo and Ficus malacocarpa.

*View of the atrium. Exterior view of the building covered with vegetation. Aerial view. Interior view of the offices. The glazed ground floor.*

*Exterior view of the façade.*
*Section of MIA Design Studio Office.*

# Factory in the Earth

## JOHOR | MALAYSIA

**Architect: Ryuichi Ashizawa Architects & associates**
**Year: 2013**
**Landscape area: 27,143 m$^2$**
**Further participants:**
**Inada Junichi, Robert Yiew, Hirokazu Toki**
**Technical features:**
**Reinforced concrete structure with brick wall construction. Use of native greenery to blend the building into its surroundings.**

This expansion of an existing factory in Johor, Malaysia, redefines industrial architecture. Instead of a purely functional construction, it created a harmonious transition between building and jungle, integrating nature and establishing an inspiring work environment for employees. The building's roof forms a green continuation of the earth's surface, improves heat insulation, and minimizes energy consumption. A structure made of hexagonal pillars with star-shaped capitals – inspired by arabesque patterns and the surrounding vegetation – carries the room beneath it. Integrated pipes guide rainwater into an underground tank, where it is used to water the plants and provide natural cooling for the interior space. To optimize the use of daylight, specially designed panels reflect the incident light, making artificial lighting largely unnecessary. The multi-story office unit runs along the east-west axis to reduce direct sunlight. A wraparound ramp connects all stories and makes the structure accessible on foot. Green façades with climbing plants protect against the heat, while natural ventilation is enhanced through the elevation difference between the office and production areas. This sustainable factory unites industrial efficiency with ecological sensibility and creates architecture that seamlessy blends into its tropical surroundings.

Number of species: 32. Plants mainly used: Shorea, Tristania, Alstonia, Cyrtostachys renda, Caryota mitis.

*Exterior view of the tower covered with vegetation. Interior view. Interior view of the roof. View of the climbing plants surrounding the tower. Floor plan. Design concept. Sections.*

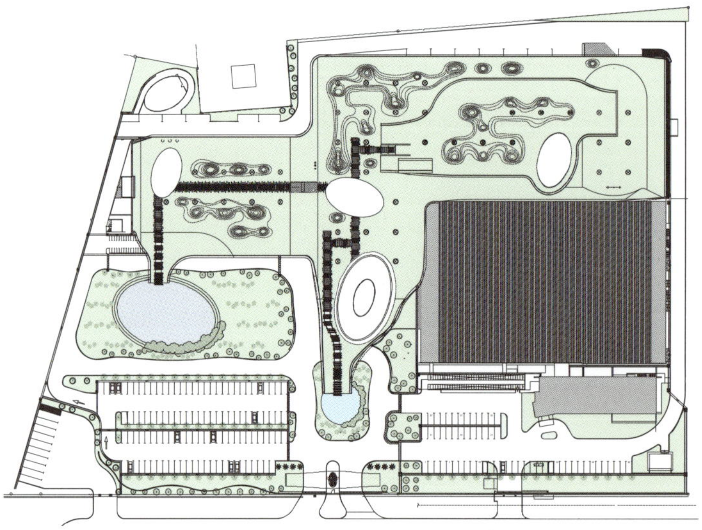

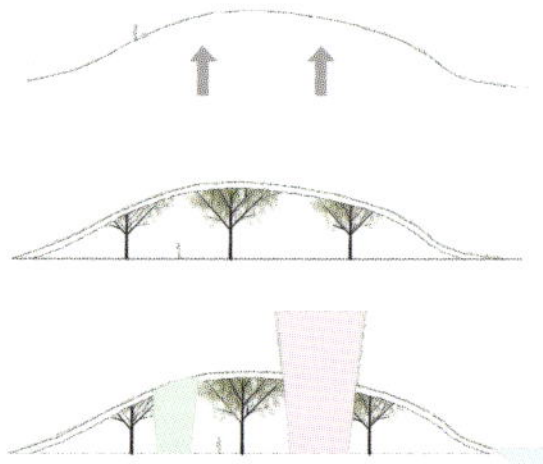

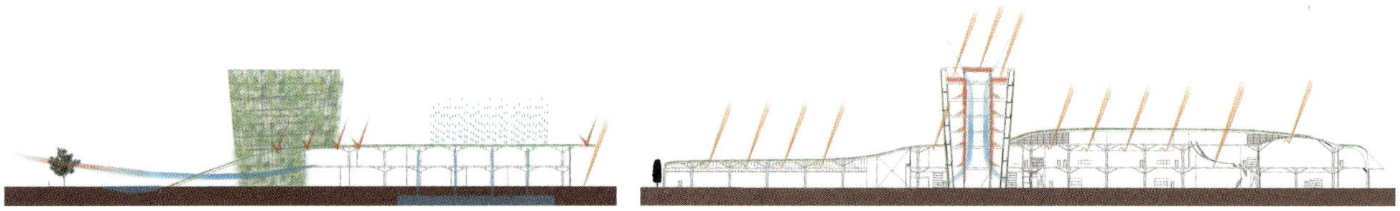

*Exterior view of the entire building. View of the green roof integrated into the surrounding nature.*

# Regenbogen-wald

## DARMSTADT | GERMANY

**Architect: blrm Architekt*innen**
**Year: in construction, completion scheduled for the end of 2027**
**Area: 2,250 m²**
**Further participants:**
**rabe Landschaften, knippershelbig**
**Technical features:**
**Circular construction. Reused building materials.**

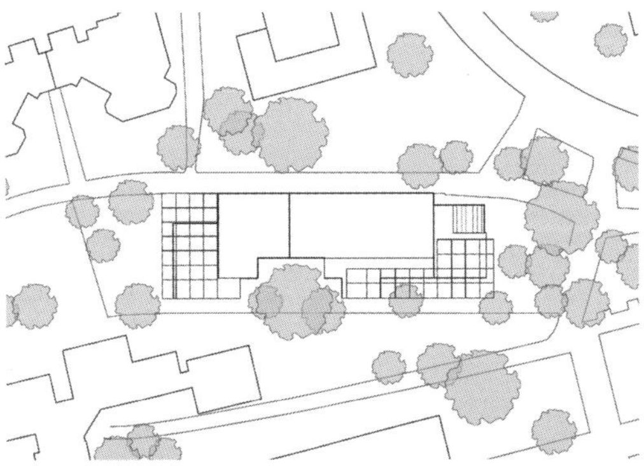

A large number of residential building projects are emerging in Darmstadt's Verlegerviertel district, resulting in a need to expand the social infrastructure. On the plot that was once home to a daycare center, a new build is replacing the old, dilapidated building. The new structure will also offer space for a youth center and other social offerings, serving as an important social hub for residents. The project's goal is to use exclusively existing building parts from the dismantled structures. This will help save resources and avoid waste. The process involves taking material that is no longer required at a specific location and reusing it at a different site, saving on gray energy and honoring the beauty of what already exists. The architecture supports the pedagogical approach, which is why the interconnection between the interior and exterior spaces represents a particularly significant element. The existing garden shapes the new building's contextualization and design. As the search for new construction parts continues, the design of building changes in an evolving process. The patchwork image, in the sense of a bricolage, serves as a guiding principle in developing the future structure's expressiveness. The impact of the reused building elements extends beyond simply recycling materials and establishes a connection between the past, present, and future.

Number of species: 19. Plants mainly used: Pinus nigra, Juglans regia, Prunus avium, Acer pseudoplatanus, Castanea sativa, Ulmus laevis.

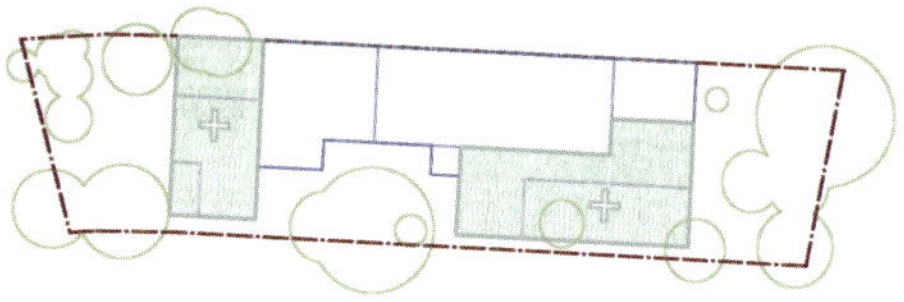

*Floor plan. Exterior view of the building. Scheme of tree preservation and new green scaffolding. Drawing of the interior. Floor plans.*

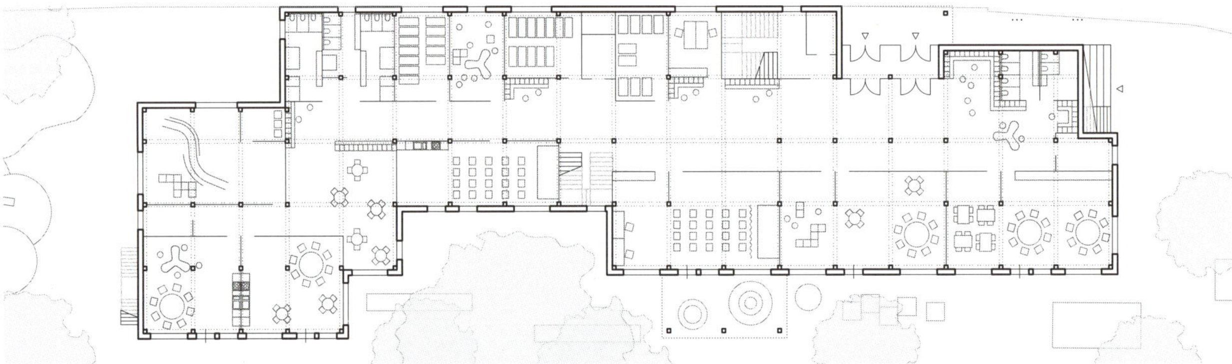

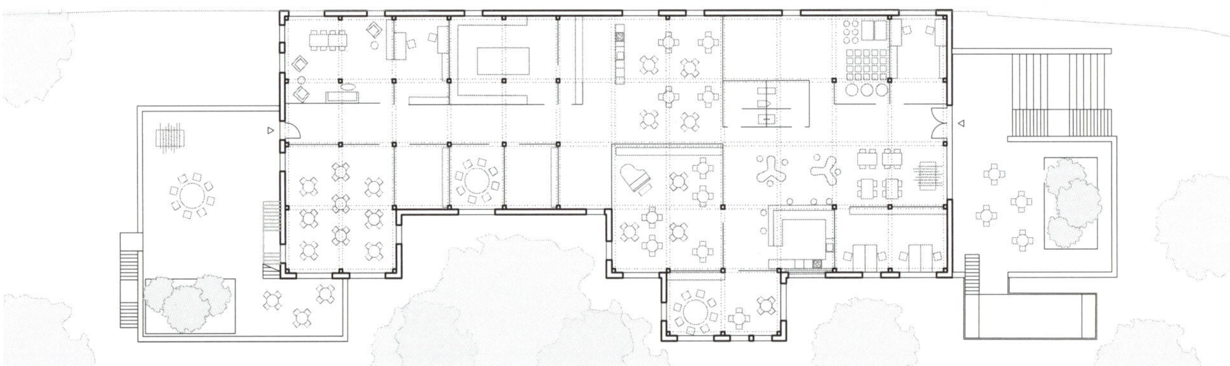

*Drawing of the building from the outside. Axonometrie.*

# COAF Guest House

## LORI PROVINCE | ARMENIA

**Architect: Studio Paul Kaloustian**
**Year: 2019**
**Area: 600 m²**
**Technical features:**
**Concrete structure. Glass façades.**
**Roof as part of the landscape.**

COAF Guest House, part of the Smart Campus in the northern Armenian town of Debet, harmoniously slots into the gently sloping landscape. A striking, sheer rampart, marking the entrance to the guest house, unfolds upon entering: it softens and stretches into the landscape that spreads out behind its long glass façade. The usual amenities of a guest house – bedroom, lobby, restaurant – seamlessly adapt to the topographical circumstances. Every room opens up towards nature via the glass façade, while the back is used for linear access and accommodates additional areas. The flat roof is the project's characteristic element: as a "nonexistent" roof, it blends into the environment with its soil covering and thereby recreates the original topography. This turns the guest house into an independent expansion of the terrain that respects the scenery and doesn't compete with it. The architecture displays a respectful dialog between the building and Armenia's beautiful scenery.

Plants mainly used: wild grass.

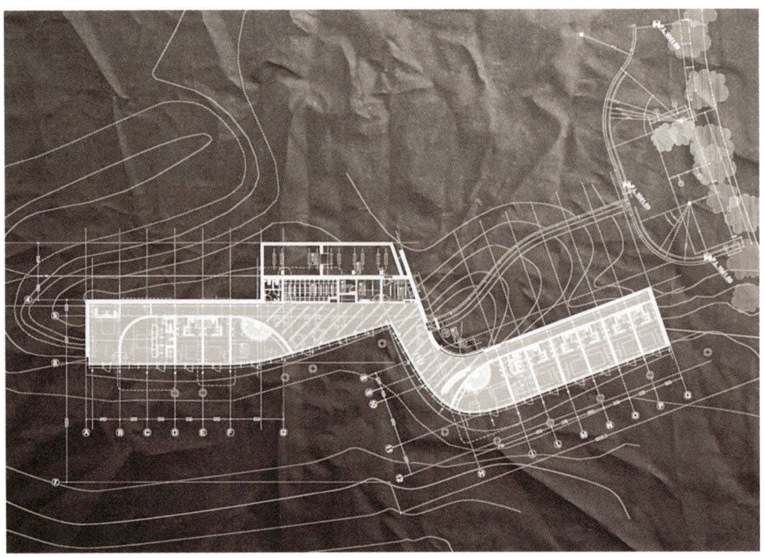

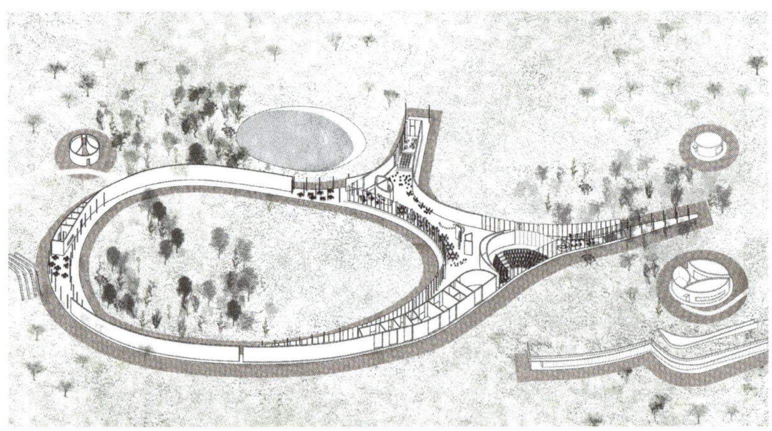

*Exterior view from the surrounding landscape. Interior view. Lobby with panoramic windows. View of the grass-covered building. Interior view. Floor plan. Axonometry. Exterior view of the green roof.*

# Cool Shadow Office

## VIENNA | AUSTRIA

**Architect: RATAPLAN - Architektur ZT**
**Year: 2016**
**Area: 800 m² green façade**
**Further participants:**
**Vienna University of Natural Resources and Life Sciences (BOKU), Schöberl & Pöll GmbH, GB-Consult**
**Technical features:**
**Thermal restoration of the façade. Green support structure with steel columns, planters and trellises.**

The goal was to complete a thermal restoration of a radical, very vertically structured south/west façade of the MA31's administrative office, built in the 1960's, and combine it with a new green function or structure. The rhythm of the relief, consisting of lesenes, parapets, and window planes, has largely been preserved and is reinforced by a support structure comprising steel columns placed on their own foundation, planters, and trellises. The offset planters, offering a generous root area and sun protection from above, give rise to a new pattern together with the existing vertical structure. This provides the opportunity to use creepers and climbing plants that can grow beyond the story heights on trellises. The trellises are designed in such a way that they provide perfect support for the plants. Visually, they also structure the façade in an attractive way even when it isn't covered in plants. By adding evergreen climbers, the lateral shading will still partially exist in the winter. The plants and planters enable optimal shade while offering a clear view. A controlled irrigation system with remote monitoring completes the sustainable concept. BOKU, the Vienna University of Natural Resources and Life Sciences, and the Vienna University of Technology monitored the building for three years and found that the vegetation developed well. In 2018, the climbing plants achieved 24% greater coverage than the size of the green area. All in all, they stored 480 kg of $CO^2$, equal to the emissions of a car travelling 2,300 km.

*Exterior view of the façade. The building from the street. View of the new exterior structure.*

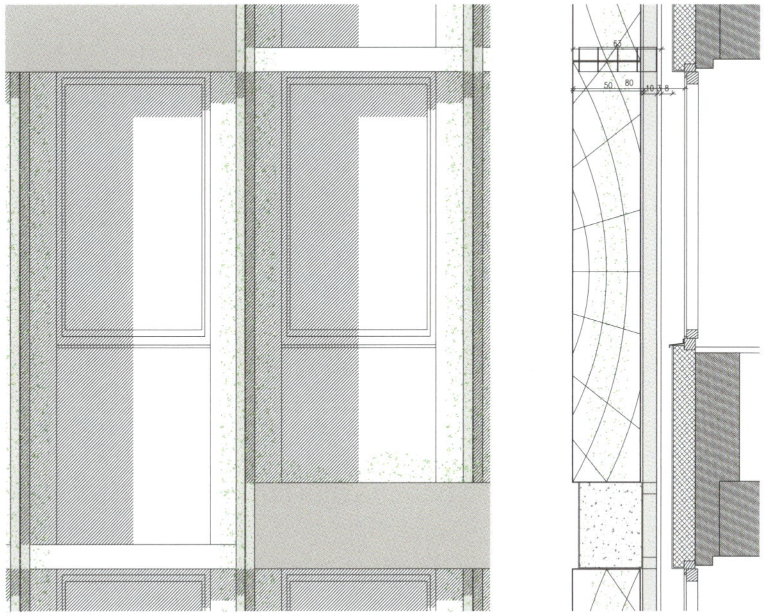

*Exterior façade covered by the plans. Elevation and section of the new façade structure.*

Number of species: 5 climbing plants, 7 perennials, 2 bulbs. Plants mainly used: Akebia quinata, Aristolochia macrophylla, Lonicera tellmanniana, Lonicera henryi, Wisteria floribunda, Iris "Interpol".

# VanDusen Botanical Garden Visitor Centre

## BRITISH COLUMBIA | CANADA

**Architect: Perkins&Will**
**Year: 2011**
**Area: 1,765 m$^2$**
**Further participants:**
**Sharp & Diamond Landscape Architecture with Cornelia Hahn Oberlander, Raincoast Applied Ecology, Fast + Epp**
**Technical features:**
**Traditional non-inverted green roof.**

The Visitor Centre in the VanDusen Botanical Garden was not just designed in response to nature but also reflects its shapes and processes. Inspired by organic structures and natural systems, the building strives for a harmonious balance between architecture and landscape – both visually and ecologically. As the first Living Building Challenge (LBC)-certified project in Canada, it exceeds the LEED Platinum Standard and meets the highest standards for sustainability in the building industry. The building uses on-site renewable energy sources – geothermic drilling, solar panels, and solar thermal energy – to achieve net-zero energy consumption every year. Rainwater is filtered and used to cover the building's gray-water requirements; all blackwater is treated on site in a bioreactor and discharged into a newly created seepage field and a garden. Natural ventilation is aided by a solar-powered fireplace that turns sunrays into convection energy. In the summer, solar radiation on dark surfaces also supports ventilation. The building's roof consists entirely of FSC-certified Douglas fir wood and is comprised of 71 prefabricated panels. These are equipped with heat insulation, sprinkler systems, light channels, soundproofing material, and wooden ceiling strips. The use of wood as the main building material offers another ecological advantage: it stores enough carbon dioxide to make the project climate neutral. The VanDusen Visitor Centre presents pioneering architecture that engages in a dialog with nature and meets the highest sustainability standards.

Number of species: ca. 50. Plants mainly used:
Garry oak, Pacific madrone, River birch, Saskatoon.
Shrubs: Kinnikinnick, Red huckleberry, Slough sedge.

*Exterior view of the green roof. The outer roof from below. View from the entrance. Interior view. The Visitor Centre at night.*

*Exterior view of the building from the surrounding garden.*
*Floor plan.*

# Bi House Nha Trang

## NHA TRANG CITY | VIETNAM

**Architect: Pham Huu Son Architects**
**Year: 2022**
**Area: 250 m²**
**Further participants:**
**NHA XANH 79 Company**
**Technical features:**
**Climbing Green. Green roof.**

Bi House in Nha Trang unites sustainable design with a tropical quality of life. Spanning just 80 square meters, it offers a green retreat that interweaves nature with the living space and thereby reduces the human impact on the environment. Vertical greenery infuses the architecture, serving as natural protection from heat, noise, and dust, while also giving the house a striking, organic aesthetic. In light of Vietnam's tropical climate, natural ventilation is prioritized. The main bedroom sits beneath a green roof and stays pleasantly cool, whereas a deep air lane between the two bedrooms on the middle floor diverts heat. This runs from the ground floor all the way up to the roof terrace and creates a second protective wall against direct sunlight. In addition, horizontal ventilation slits behind and above the staircase regulate the air circulation in the entire building. Lush gardens are another natural cooling factor, surrounding the house and guiding fresh air into the living space. They act as a green lung and create a harmonious connection between the interior and exterior areas. The lighting concept also follows sustainable principles: strategically placed glazing maximizes daylight penetration and reduces power consumption. This results in a bright, breezy atmosphere that merges energy efficiency with a tropical living experience – a successful example of green architecture in Southeast Asia.

Number of species: 80. Plants mainly used: Indian barringtonia, Apanese fan palm, Split philodendron leaf, Carambola, Barbados cherry tree.

*Balcony covered with plants.*
*Main view. Bi House from above.*
*Bathtub open to the terrace.*
*Top view of the swimming pool.*

*Panoramic views from the master bedroom surrounded by vegetation. Bi House concept. Floor plans.*

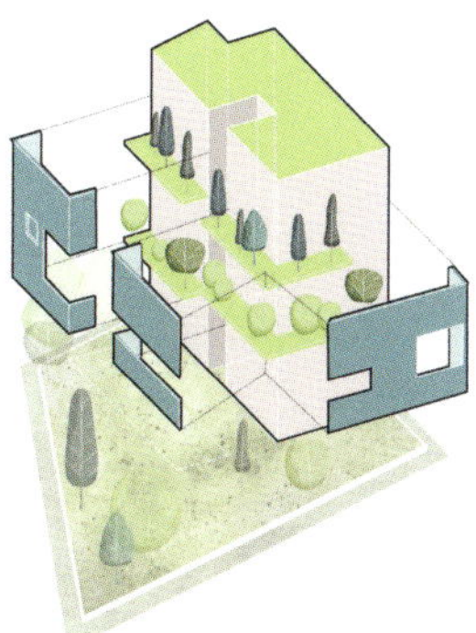

# ARABELLA 26

## MUNICH | GERMANY

**Architect: Aika Schluchtmann, Schluchtmann Architekten**
**Year: planned**
**Area: 8,600 m²**
**Further participants: Vertical greening Vertiko**
**Technical features: Plant troughs standing on cantilever plates with drip irrigation and stainless steel netting as a climbing aid.**

A vertical garden for Munich – biodiversity on 16 levels. In the middle of the visionary district of Arabellapark from the 1960's, a green high rise emerges, designed by Schluchtmann Architekten from Munich. The attractive freestanding building with 16 stories and a horizontal mixture of uses strengthens the urbanistic identity and creates a seamless transition to the neighboring high rises. The building plays with the amorphous and free building shape of the adjacent Arabeska building and adds a green high point to this building complex, turning it into an effective triad of urban planning. The façade, featuring over 2,000 m² of greenery, constitutes the core of the design. Approximately 1,200 climbing plants, trailing from one story to the next, form the vertical garden of this 52-meter-high freestanding building. The expansive greenery could provide a solution to the severe heat build-up in our cities. The most important task performed by these plants is that of increasing the humidity, which leads to evaporative cooling. Greenery reduces the heat radiation, minimizes heat reflection, and thereby improves the microclimate. In addition, the façade acts as natural air purifier by binding fine dust and produces oxygen and $CO^2$. Different plants are used in different parts of building, such as vine honeysuckle or Alpine clematis. This directly contributes to the preservation of biodiversity and can serve as a strategy to compensate for the loss of green spaces in areas with high urban density.

*Exterior view of the building covered with vegetation. Arabella 26 from above. Main view.*

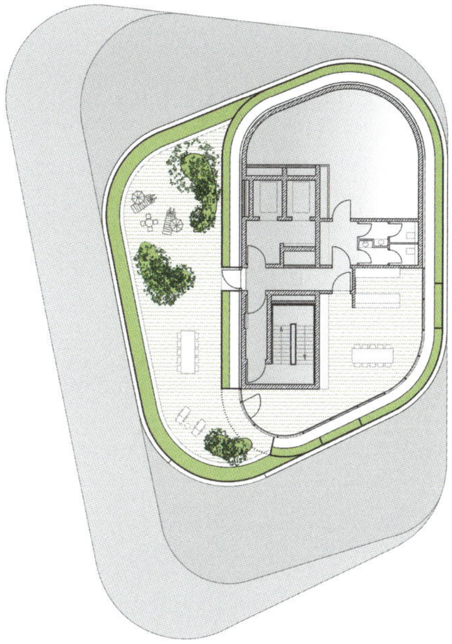

*View of the building from the street. Top floor with shared roof terrace. Detail of the façade.*

Number of species: ca. 25. Plants mainly used: medium-growing, robust climbing plants without light-flying shoots.

# The Coconut Club & Park

## PHNOM PENH | CAMBODIA

**Architect: KANOPEA ARCHITECTURE STUDIO / T3 ARCHITECTS**
**Year: 2021**
**Area: 1,800 m$^2$**
**Technical features:**
**Bioclimatic Principles. Low-tech solutions. Biophilic façade.**

The Coconut Club & Park comprises a city park and a building constructed with ecology and sustainability in mind. It contains rooms for conferences, catering, education, and well-being. In light of its urban setting in southeast Asia, the architects' goal was to restrict the building's surface area, gain as many natural spaces as possible, and create a real park in which the ground that could absorb rain – thereby preventing heat islands and combating the risk of flooding. The compact architecture is designed in line with bioclimatic (sun protection, natural ventilation, protection against monsoon rains, etc.) and biophilic (predominant presence of plants) principles. This well-thought-out low-tech solution is affordable, emits low amounts of carbon dioxide, and offers optimal comfort. 80% of the building's rooms do not have air-conditioning, which reduces energy consumption significantly compared to a "normal" building. Vernonia elliptica in the overhanging planters forms a protective "green curtain" that helps cool the building passively. In combination with the trees and plants on the ground surrounding the building, this creates a green environment that offers protection against the sun and has a refreshing effect. At the same time, gardeners have an easy job caring for them. In addition, this lends the project a unique aesthetic that has already turned it into a popular place for Cambodians to relax, train, or eat.

Plants mainly used: Epipremnum aureum, Musa acuminata, Vernonia elliptica as protective "green curtain".

*View of the building covered with greenery. Interior view. Front view of the green façade. Interior view. Floor plan.*

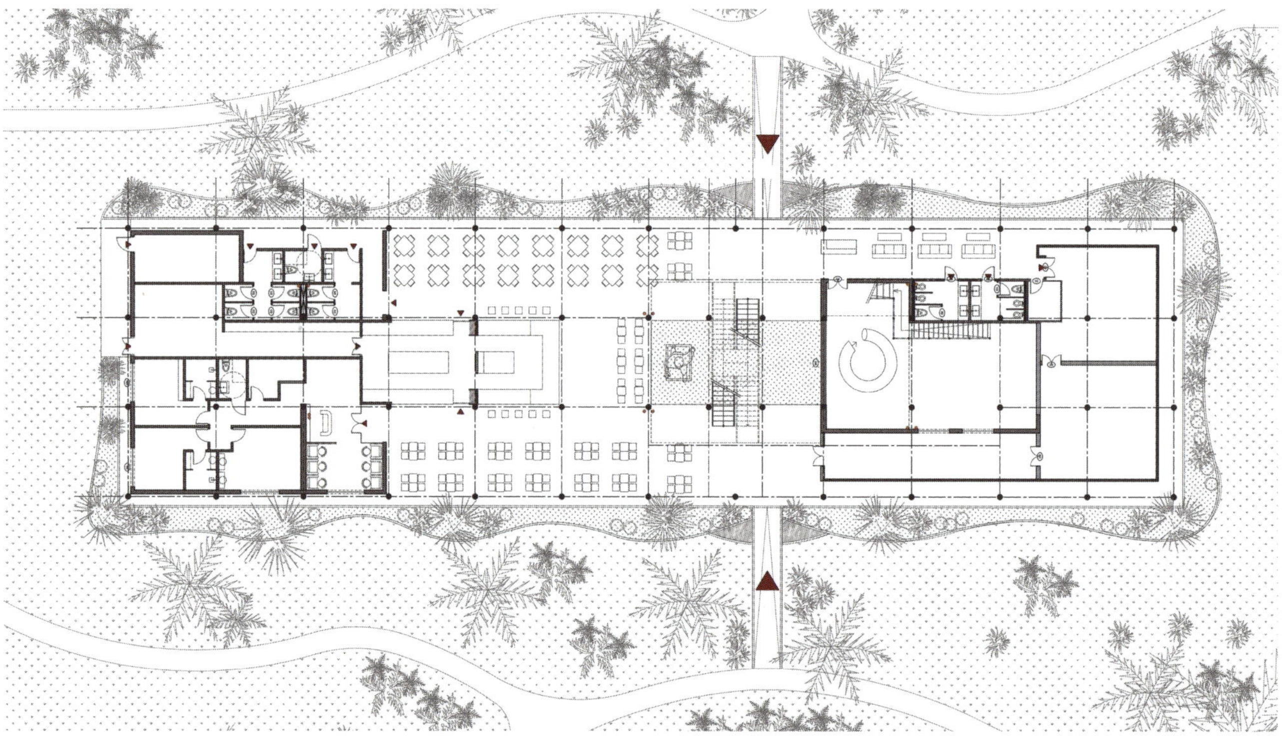

*Side view of the green building surrounded by the garden. View of the staircase.*

# 124

# IKEA the good neighbour

## VIENNA | AUSTRIA

**Architect: querkraft**
**Year: 2021**
**Area: 29,480 m²**
**Further participants:**
**Kräftner Landschaftsarchitektur, Green4Cities**
**Technical features:**
**External shell as shelves with space for greenery and terraces. Prefabricated reinforced concrete columns for more flexible spaces.**

As the worlds first car free IKEA the building makes a significant contribution to the future of a lively and ecological city and to the future of retail – this urban IKEA features excellent public transport links, a roof terrace, and a neighborly attitude. The developer had already made this explicitly clear in the briefing: "We want to be a good neighbor". The solution provided by querkraft depicts a building that also represents added value for the surrounding area. On the publicly accessible rooftop, visitors can sip coffee, relax, and enjoy the view of the city and the plentiful greenery. All of this contributes to the store's status of "good neighbor". The 4.5-meter-wide exterior zone surrounds the building like a shady shelf. It allows for room extensions, offers space for terraces and plants, plus service elements such as lifts, emergency stairways, and building services. Putting all the infrastructure in the outer shell is key for the flexible use of space on the inside of the building. The entry level is a lively place – a spacious airspace connects it to the retail areas at the front. Inside, a continuous airspace offers unimpeded views between the different stories. 160 trees in the façade and on the roof noticeably impact the microclimate. The climbing plants and trees of the IKEA furniture store have a cooling and humidifying effect – natural air-conditioning. This also improves the air temperature on the pedestrian level. Computer simulations resulted in a relevant temperature reduction of 1.5°C. To ensure the building's efficient conditioning, the housing technology is based on a simple principle – short distances and direct access. The prefabricated reinforced concrete stilts follow a grid of about 10 x 10 meters, which allows for versatile use and design of the rooms. The lower floors accommodate IKEA Retail, while the top two levels house the Jo&Joe hostel with 345 beds. This mixture has created a house that's alive day and night.

IKEA

Plants mainly used: climbing plants and trees.

*Perspective from above. Main view from the street. Interior view. Detail of the façade. Section. Roof plan.*

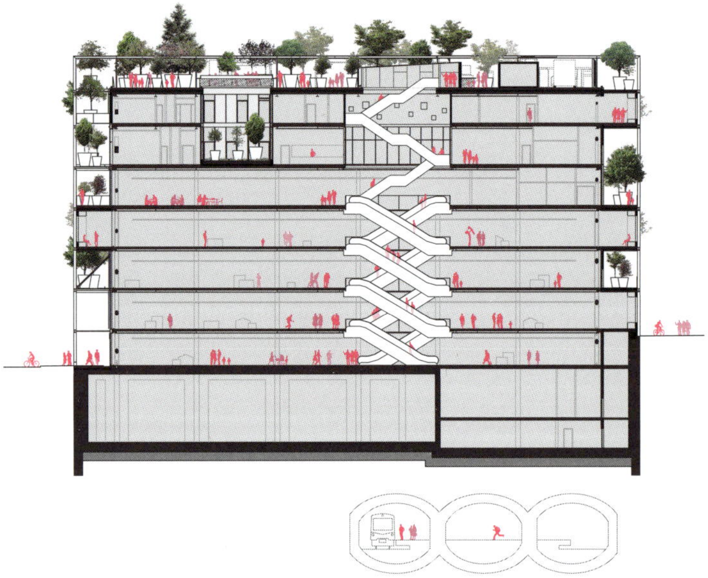

*Exterior front view.*
*View from the rooftop.*

# Touching Eden House

## SINGAPORE | REPUBLIC OF SINGAPORE

**Architect: Wallflower Architecture + Design**
**Year: 2023**
**Area: 1,300 m²**
**Further participants:**
**MSE Consultants, ALLZ Consulting Services, Salad Dressing, Light Collab, Edmund Ng Interior Studio, Nyee Phoe Flower Garden, Cubo, Giorgetti Asia, Sapphire Windows, Soluzioni, Otiima, Good Class Builders**
**Technical features:**
**Grid façade and vegetation as screening.**

Touching Eden House is an oasis of peace and tranquility, embedded in the lush greenery at the edge of the Singapore Botanic Gardens, the city's first UNESCO World Heritage Site. The brief called for a typical family house. A biophilic pavilion on stilts served as inspiration, surrounded by lattices and nestled into sumptuous plant life that harmoniously blends into the borders of the botanical garden. The garden was designed as an expansion of the botanical garden and the plants were selected accordingly. The building's exterior offers a modern privacy screen and sun protection, supported by clear lines and large glass windows that open up to a breathtaking view of the enclosing greenery. Natural materials such as travertine, granite and high-quality timber harmonize with the environment. Large, open-plan rooms and ceiling-high windows let in plenty of natural light. The office and gym, strategically positioned on the top floor, offer a panorama of the surrounding treetops. Hanging plants, draping from the roof terrace and down the sides of the house, act as a green curtain. A layer of accoya envelops the top level, serving as a privacy screen and sun protection. The grid façade consists of various vertical sections that can be arranged flexibly in 12 different combinations. As a result, a number of diagonal surfaces can capture the sunlight at different times of day, create unique shadows, and amplify the light effects.

## Plants mainly used: Lee kuan yew creeper, Maiden's jealousy / Galphimia vine, Pink mempat, Syzygium gratum, Lagerstroemia langkawiensis.

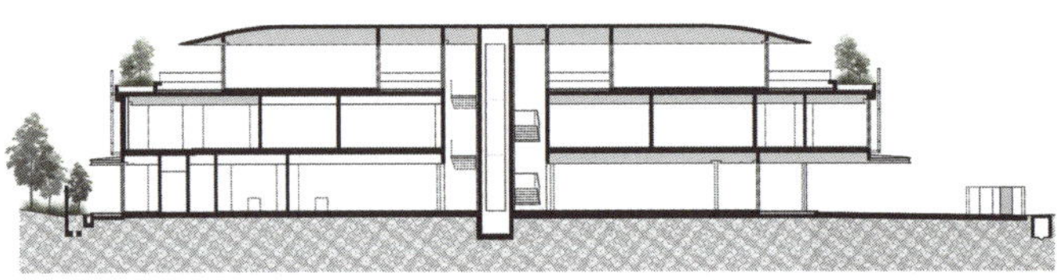

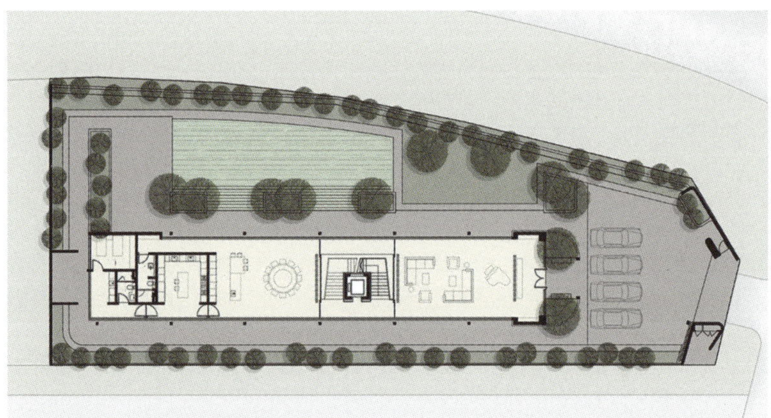

*Exterior view of the building from the garden. Green façade. Exterior of the building covered with vegetation. View of one terrace. Cross section. Longitudinal section. Floor plan.*

*Exterior view of the building at night. Interior view of a terrace covered with vegetation.*

# Holiday home by Þingvallavatn

## ÞINGVALLAVATN | SOUTHWESTERN ICELAND

**Architect: KRADS**
**Year: 2020**
**Area: 145 m²**
**Technical features:**
**Green roof. Natural ventilation. Mainly locally sourced materials.**

The holiday home was carefully placed on an overgrown hill in southwestern Iceland, gently leading northwards to the impressive Þingvallavatn. The building's shape follows the topographical structure of the landscape, which inspired the multi-level design. In harmony with the terrain, the concrete foundation of the timber structure spans three offset levels that trace the movement of the hill. The roof, covered with local grass and moss, partially slopes towards the hill and follows its form. The house's placement was chosen with care to integrate the building into its surroundings harmoniously and at the same time create special vistas. In the north, the house rises above the low shrubbery and opens up to an unobstructed view of the Þingvallavatn and Skjaldbreið. On the opposite side, the main room leads out to a southwest-facing terrace, surrounded by trees. From here, the Jórutindur and Hátindur mountains are visible, and the panorama stretches through the house and all the way to the lake. With the exception of the terrace, the house's immediate surroundings are so overgrown that they appear almost inaccessible. Preserving the original landscape was one of the key concerns during the design process and construction phase. To compensate for this, the green roof is used as an accessible level. Access is provided either via the house's interior, from the sleeping and playing gallery, or from the outside, where the slope begins at the foot of the boathouse. The roof reveals a breathtaking, constantly changing panorama of the lake and the surrounding mountains.

134

*Exterior view of the house surrounded by nature. Front view. Interior view. Exterior detail.*

*View from above of the green roof. Floor plan.*

## Number of species: 3. Plants mainly used: local turf, moss and heather.

136

# Matorral

## MEDELLÍN | COLOMBIA

**Architect: ALH Taller**
**Year: 2017**
**Area: 548 m²**
**Further participants:**
**Alejandro Molina, Luis Gonzalo Moscoso, Oblicuo**
**Technical features:**
**Concrete frame structure with small overhangs. Manholes for bathroom ventilation. Irrigation system for the flowerbeds and water collection.**

In times of far-reaching environmental crises and climate change, green has become a symbol of salvation. Matorral is an architectural and constructive proposal that takes this topic very seriously. The slabs are turned into large containers with more than a hundred tropical plant species. Drip irrigation provides this little ecosystem with water in an economic fashion. This real garden, which is integrated into the structure, allows residents to enjoy the vegetation growing in the ground from inside. It gives them the feeling of being in a house from which a lush garden stretches outside. This applies to all rooms. For example, plants such as aloe vera, pencas, rosemary, thyme, basil, tomatoes, and lemon trees surround the kitchen from outside. On the third floor, a lost squirrel is a common sight, leaping from one of the tree's branches and entering the building through the windows. From the outside, Matorral has basically engulfed the façade. It has become a little oasis in the city's concrete heart.

Number of species: 50. Plants mainly used: Aloe vera to rosemary, Thyme, Basil, Tomatoes and Lemon trees.

*View from the balcony to the surrounding nature. Night view. View of the building covered with plants. View from the terrace. Interior view.*

*Exterior front view. View from above. Section.*

# Max-Planck-Institut

## HAMBURG | GERMANY

**Landscape Architect: Landschaftsarchitektur+ Holzapfel-Herziger & Benesch**
**Year: 2022**
**Area: ca. 2,500 m² of roof garden**
**Further participants:**
**Mark Krieger, Hammeskrause Architekten**
**Technical features:**
**Intensive and extensive greening in multiple layers with drainage. Connection to cistern for irrigation automation and grey water use.**

The three-story Max-Planck-Institut for the Structure and Dynamics of Matter is a complex scientific building for basic research on matter, situated on an expansive science campus in Hamburg. The green park landscape on the roof provides a place to escape the research work that takes place in light-deprived laboratories. The terracing of the 150-meter-long building gives rise to roof areas at different levels. The upper roof areas, used for technical superstructures, feature extensive greenery. They were enriched with flowering shrubs to provide more nourishment for insects. On the lower roof areas, a natural-looking park landscape invites visitors to stay a while. Thanks to the ramps and staircases that provide access from the outside, employees from the neighboring institute can also take advantage of the roof garden, making it an attractive meeting place for the scientific community on the campus. Corresponding with the meandering routing above the roof areas, planted areas were designed with wave-like bands of vegetation, consisting of perennials, grasses, and shrubs. Different colored shrubs that rise up from the inner courtyards connect the floor levels visually and offer attractive inside and outside views. Planning particularly focused on the aspect of water circulation. Thanks to the substrate thickness and water retention boards with high retention volume, the planting system can store a particularly large amount of rainwater. Excess precipitation is diverted into a cistern. From there, this precipitation is reused for irrigation and as gray water in the building.

Number of species: 75. Plants mainly used: Ironwood tree, Copper rock pear, Shrub forest pine, various perennials.

*Exterior view of the roof garden.*
*Aerial view of the entire building.*
*View of the roof garden paths.*
*Exterior view. Shaped benches.*

*Top view of the Max-Planck-Institut.*
*Exterior view. Longitudinal section.*
*Axonometrie.*

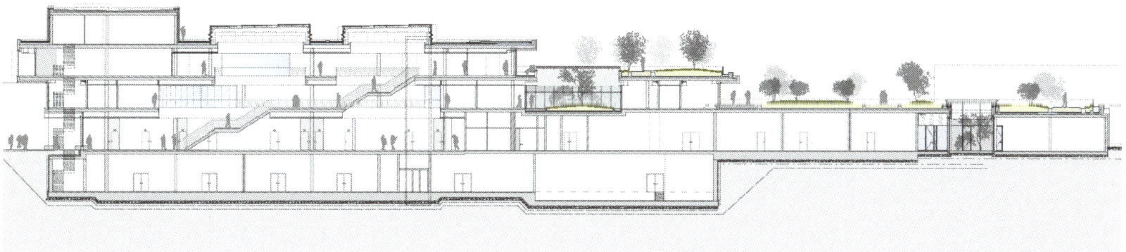

144

# Writer's Shed

## MELBOURNE | AUSTRALIA

**Architect: Matt Gibson Architecture & Design**
**Year: 2016**
**Area: 9.9 m$^2$**
**Further participants:**
**Ben Scott Garden Design, Warwick Constructions**
**Technical features:**
**Passive techniques of site orientation and cross-ventilation. Double-glazed Low-E glass.**

Camouflaged and nestled in a modest residential garden, the Writer's Shed serves as a retreat for creative work in the garden of a home in southeastern Melbourne. The small structure is placed in a rarely used corner of the quiet property and blends in with the surrounding natural environment. Boston ivy and lush plants, developed in collaboration with landscape designer Ben Scott, turn the pavilion into a lively part of the garden. The inside reveals a puristic, plywood-clad office space. A large window frames the view of the greenery, while a mirrored door leads to the bluestone-paved lane at the back – a discreet entrance for deliveries. The dimensions of ten square meters were chosen so that the shed would fall into the category of a Class 10a structure, enabling a cost-efficient, minimalist implementation. A concrete foundation supports the wooden flooring. The walls consist of plywood and feature a butynol coating on the outside, acting as both insulation and a seal. In times of constant change to our ways of working and living, the Writer's Shed offers an alternative to the hectic, interconnected office world. It creates an intimate space to retreat, reflect, and develop innovative ideas – a serene refuge amidst the greenery.

Number of species: 10. Plants mainly used: Boston ivy, Euphorbia, Star jasmine, Green pole cactus, Pratia ground cover, Oak-leaf hydrangea, Liriope.

*Exterior façade completely covered with climbing greenery. Interior view. View of the cabin entrance. Floor plan. Elevation. Section.*

*Exterior view of the cabin camouflaged in the surrounding vegetation. Interior view.*

148

# DDoffice

## HO CHI MINH CITY | VIETNAM

**Architect: DDconcept Architecture**
**Year: 2015**
**Area: 38 m²**
**Technical features:**
**Ground, wall and roof plants.**

In a metropolis characterized by a high level of construction, pollution, and a lack of green spaces, workspaces become a second home for employees. The architects' priority was to create an open-plan work environment that not only promotes interaction between colleagues but also establishes a connection with nature. Originally, they had envisioned a horizontal office design, but the limited space of just 38 square meters required a creative, vertical solution. The arrangement of the open spaces in all four cardinal directions creates a vertical link between the different levels that facilitates collaboration among employees. Thanks to large window façades, every level offers views of lush greenery, which not only provides privacy but also ensures natural light and a pleasant atmosphere. The vertical garden at the rear of the building is particularly remarkable. It acts as a green lung and helps improve the microclimate. The roof garden, equipped with a small fishpond and native plants, offers employees and visitors a place to retreat, to escape the hustle and bustle of the city. The project's design shows how a workspace can turn into a place of well-being by integrating nature, light, and fresh air.

Rooftop garden. Main view of the entrance. View of the staggered levels from below. Night view of the green façade. Axonometric view. Floor plans.

Number of species: 21. Plants mainly used: Bamboo, Her betel tree, Guava tree.

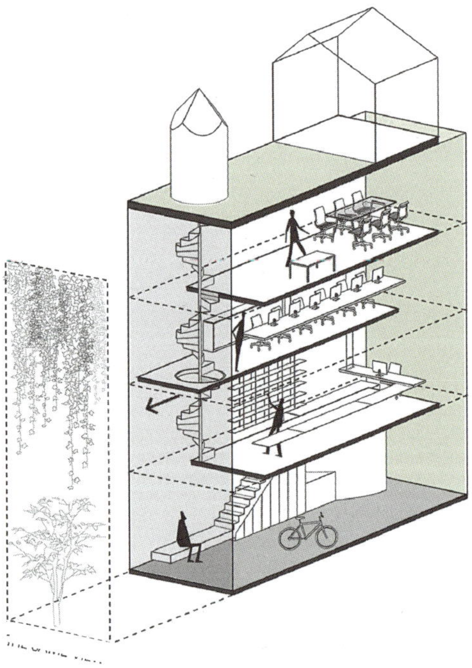

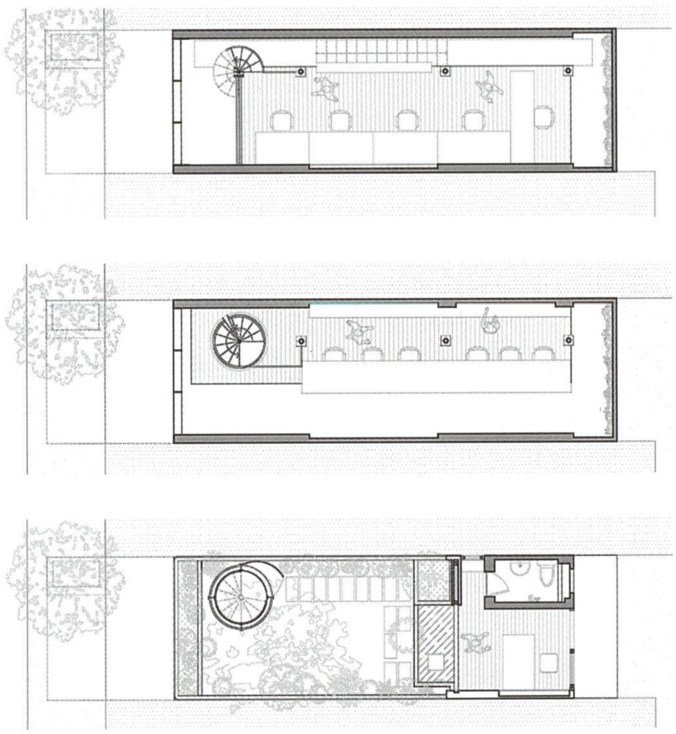

*View of the green rooftop from the working room. Interior view from above.*

# 152

# Trudo Vertical Forest

## EINDHOVEN | NETHERLANDS

**Architect: Stefano Boeri Architetti**
**Year: 2021**
**Area: 11,500 m²**
**Further participants:**
**Studio Laura Gatti, Van den Berk Nurseries, Inbo, Adviesbureau Tielemans, Ten Hooven, Du Pré Groenprojecten, Stam + De Koning Bouw**
**Technical features:**
**Prefabricated construction technologies. Green Façade. Vertical forest.**

As part of Stefano Boeri Architetti's vision for a new architecture of biodiversity, Trudo Vertical Forest was the first project for which the model of the vertical forest was applied to social housing. The project, which forms part of the "Striip-S" urban renewal plan, accommodates 125 apartments on 19 levels. These will be able to respond to future needs in a flexible way and define new standards of living. Along its four façades, the building is home to 135 trees of varying species, rising up to a height of 75 meters. In addition, about 5,200 small shrubs, plants, and other greenery grace the grounds, numbering approximately 8,500 plants in total. The building's green façades offer an effective solution for the heat-island effect. The water system is also circular: It gathers rainwater and stores it in tanks beneath the building. This is then used to irrigate the different pots. The design decisions made throughout the project particularly aimed to lower the building and maintenance costs and meet the demands of social housing. They achieved this through the use of prefabricated construction technologies and by optimizing the resources associated with planning and construction of the building. The main structure consists of prefabricated concrete modules and elements processed on site. The design of the green façade makes use of the combination of six types of pots in different shapes and sizes that are specifically used to accommodate a range of plants. It enables a variety of designs and significant reduction of costs and construction time.

Number of species: 8,500. Plants mainly used: shrubs, perennials and ground covering plants.

*Exterior view. Green façade of the Trudo Vertical Forest. Aerial view. Interior of one apartment. View from below.*

*Main view from the surrounding garden. Axonometric cutaway. Typical floor plan. Loft floor plan.*

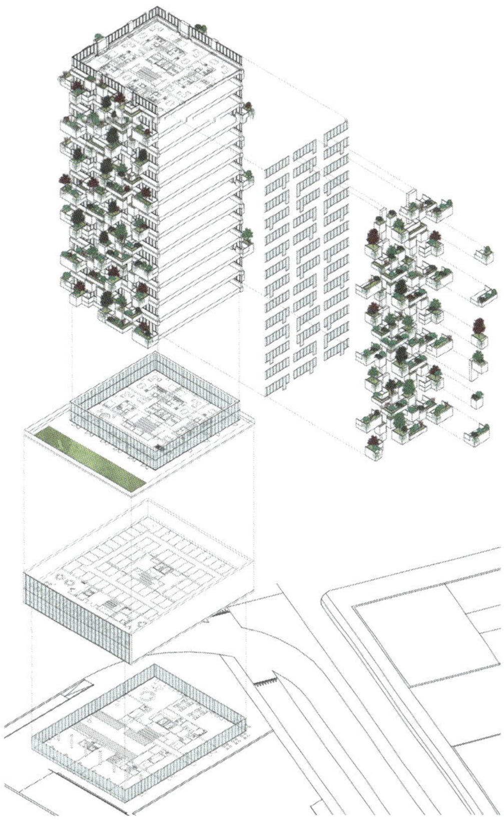

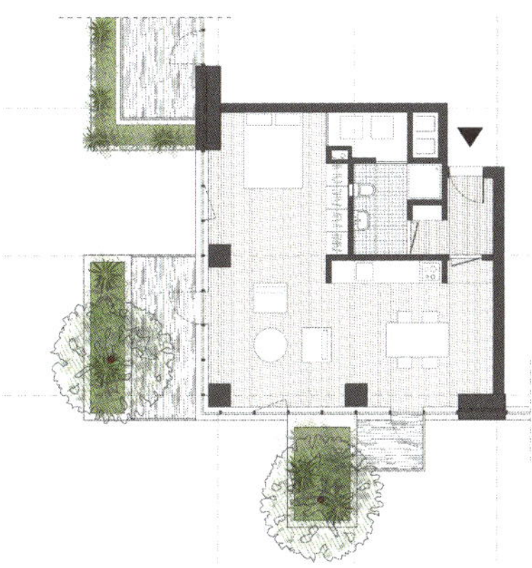

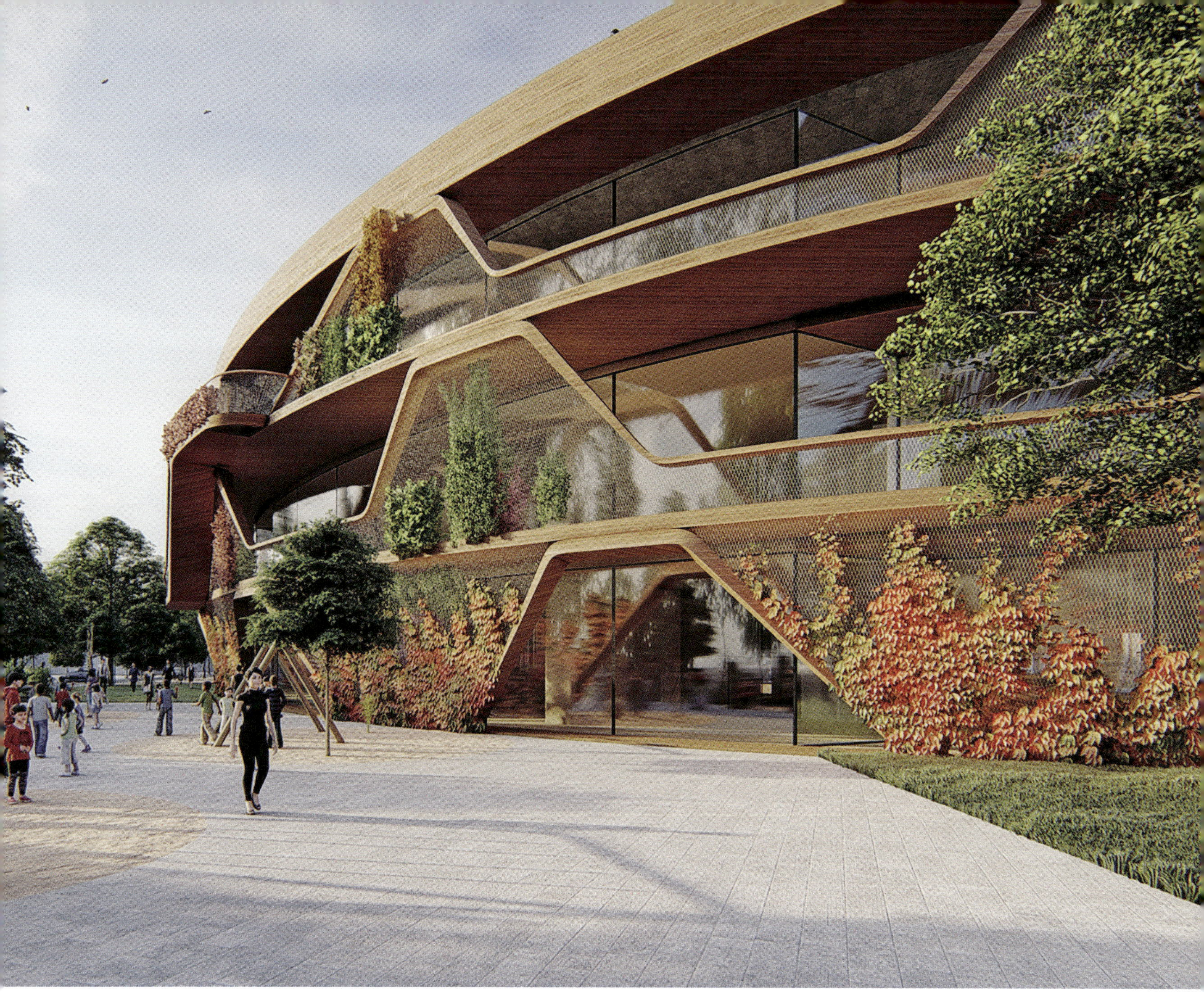

# LIFE HAMBURG

## HAMBURG | GERMANY

**Architect: LAVA - Laboratory for Visionary Architecture with Cityplot**
**Year: Feasibility study in 2020**
**Area: 19,300 m$^2$**
**Further participants:**
**Transsolar, Henning Larson Landscape, sbp, brandplus, SMV**
**Technical features:**
**Green wraparound façade. Plus-energy house. Hybrid wood construction.**

A cross-generational group of likeminded individuals gather under the same roof and share the common goal of learning. To ensure optimal conditions, the perfect learning landscape was created in an open-plan, innovative, and sustainable building. The building was developed as a three-dimensional complete system that not only enables a range of potential uses on each floor, but also vertically by introducing split levels and connecting staircases. A central agora connects the two parts of the building. This section accommodates the central facilities, such as the cafeteria and sports area. The building is largely constructed as a supporting wooden structure. With the exception of the cores with the emergency staircases and the bathrooms, the entire structure consists of solid wood elements and wooden columns, which results in an excellent carbon footprint. The building's entire envelope was developed with climate protection in mind: the generous glazed envelope offers high thermal insulation, lets plenty of daylight into the building, and establishes a link to the outdoor space. A second wraparound façade envelope features greenery, absorbs $CO^2$, and creates a refuge for animals. The greenery makes its way from the outside into the building's interior, first into the central agora and then across the open terraces and up the top floor. Wraparound terraces offer views into the green outdoor area and give students the option to learn in the fresh air. The inside and outside merge into one unit.

*Main view of the building. Aerial view. Detail of the green wraparound façade. View of the roof. General view of the building with climbing plants and edible plant garden.*

Plants mainly used: climbers, use of permaculture principles and edible landscapes.

*Exterior view of the wood and green façade. Site plan with gardens. Diagram showing floor plans.*

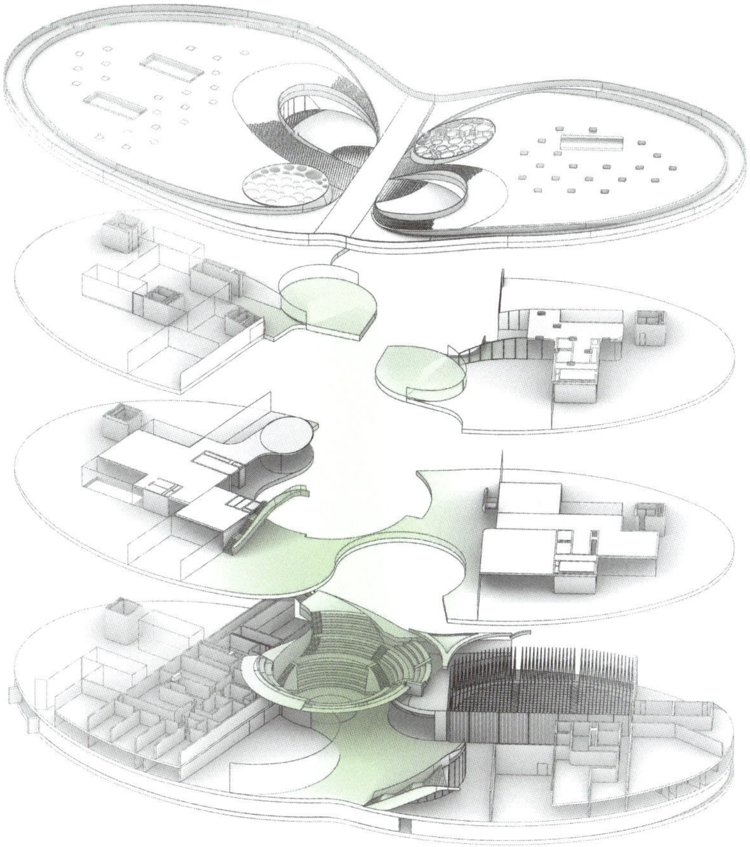

# Gurdau Winery

## KURDĚJOV | CZECH REPUBLIC

**Architect: Aleš Fiala**
**Year: 2022**
**Area: 1,141 m$^2$**
**Further participants:**
**Zdeněk Sendler Landscape, Daniela Hradilová interior design**
**Technical features:**
**Use of green roof mat Enviret Sh 30, with retention of 18-20 liters per square meter. Plants located in extensive roof substrate.**

The valley's winegrowing tradition dates back to over 1,000 years ago but vanished after World War II. The Gurdau vineyard was established on a "green meadow", with the first vines planted on the slopes above Kurdějov to revive this tradition. Symbolically, it bears the historical name of the village. The vineyard's design combines operational efficiency with aesthetic harmony. Situated centrally in the vineyards, it offers practical advantages and charming views. The gentle, wave-like curve of the building seamlessly blends into the landscape and symbolizes its unity with the natural and cultural environment. The two-story stainless-steel building comprises areas for wine production, storage, and archiving on the lower level. The ground floor serves as the wine tasting and gastronomy space and also accommodates two rental apartments to offer guests an all-round experience. The design merges traditional and contemporary elements, using materials such as exposed concrete, glass, metal, and oak and acacia wood. Large glass surfaces, terraces, and a saddle roof allow for direct contact with the landscape and open up views of Kurdějov, Pálava, and the plains towards Austria. The building is an inviting spot for social occasions, romantic moments, and quiet reflection with a glass of wine. The roof is designed as an extensive green area, while 150 shrubs and trees, some of which grow through the perforated roof surface, enrich the surroundings. Over time, this greenery will continue to embellish the scenery and contribute to its ecological value.

## Number of species: 23. Plants mainly used: Sedum (stonecrop), drought-tolerant plants and tall grasses.

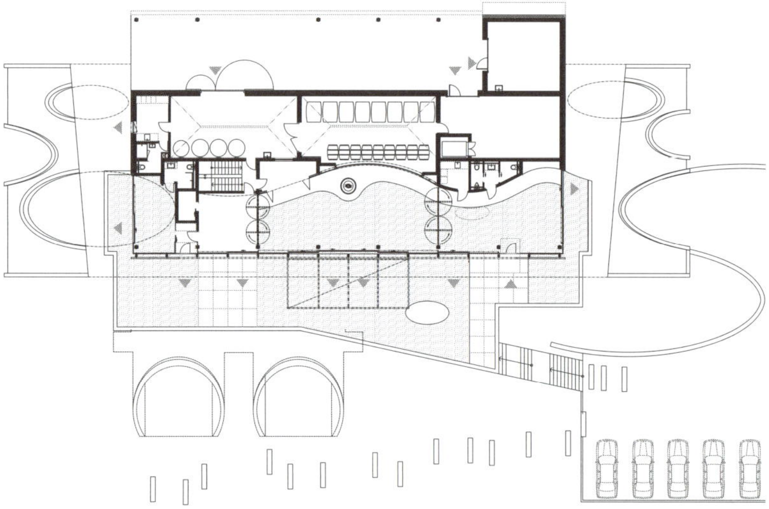

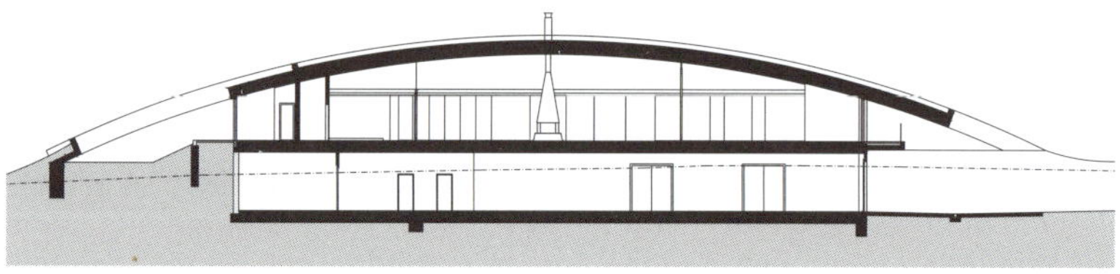

*View of the building from the surrounding greenery. Side view. View from above. Entrance to the building. Floor plan. Section.*

*Aerial view of the building fully integrated into the surrounding nature. Exterior view.*

# Yoga House

## HO CHI MINH CITY | VIETNAM

**Architect: Phạm Thanh Truyền, Phún Bảo Long and Partners**
**Year: 2022**
**Area: 780 m²**
**Further participants:**
**Cát Mộc Design & Construction, Cát Mộc Group, Pham Thanh Truyen, Phun Bao Long**
**Technical features:**
**Rough brick façade.**

Lush greenery surrounds the west-facing house, protecting the building and acting as a natural air-conditioning system. The house's "coat", which shields the structure from heat, comprises a green area that stretches from the inside to the outside, along with a brick wall with many ventilation openings. Home to a family of four, the building is situated in a densely populated district of Ho Chi Minh City. On the limited area of 185 square meters, the architects designed several gardens on every level to create an environment filled with plants. The five-story façade consists of 25,000 staggered bricks that leave "room to breathe" and block direct sunlight. To improve the microclimate and lower the temperature, the designers placed an aquarium in front of the house, surrounded by greenery. It offers residents a place to relax and enjoy the view of nature. Brown and beige tones were chosen for the interior, along with materials such as wood, glass, and concrete, to reflect the owner's minimalist and rustic taste. The first floor accommodates a communal living area with an open-plan living room, dining area, and kitchen, separated by glass walls. The bedrooms feature large balconies with plants that shield against dust and noise, while at the same time provide a natural, airy space. Since the roof and terrace absorb most of the heat, the architects envisaged a tropical garden with a vegetable patch on the terrace. A green retreat for peace and relaxation.

31/31/14

Number of species: more than 10. Plants mainly used: Ginger grass, Climbing roses, Indian chrysanthemum, Star fruit, Tuong vi tree, Bird of paradise flower.

*View of the cultivation and tropical garden on the roof. Main view of the building. Master bedroom. The aquarium surrounded by greenery. Section. Floor plans.*

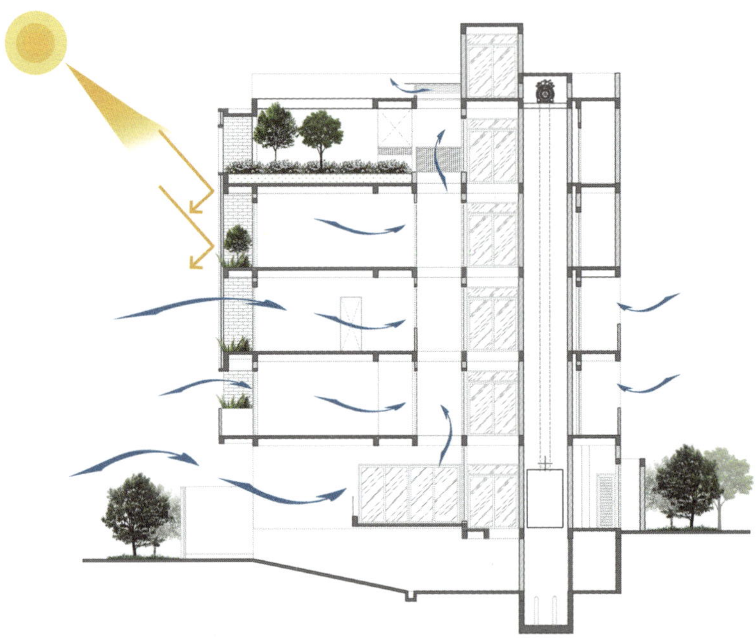

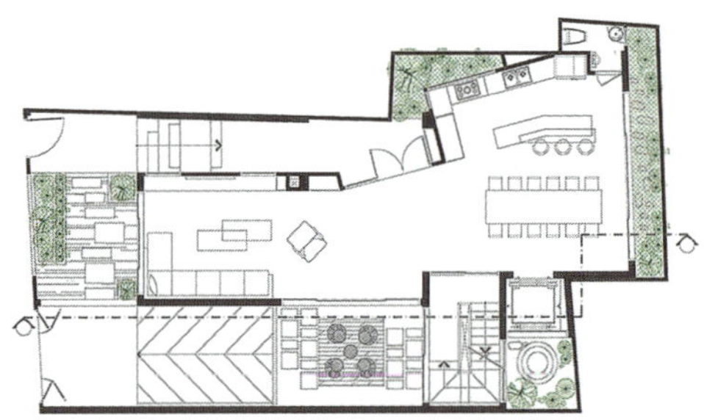

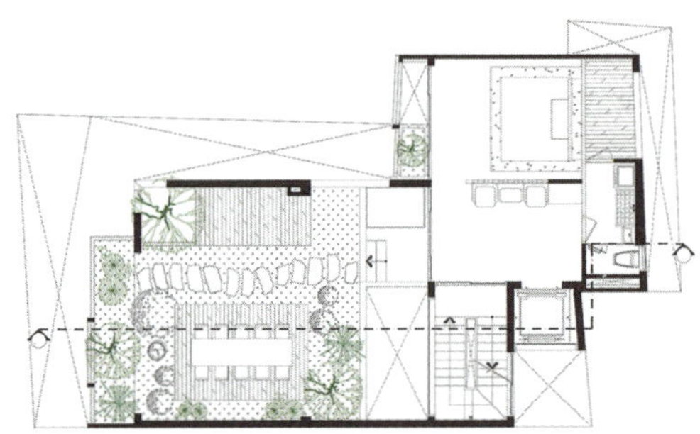

*View of the roof garden.*
*View of the staggered bricks exterior façade covered with greenery.*

# Shanghai Greenland Center

## SHANGHAI | CHINA

**Architect: Nikken Sekkei**
**Year: 2017**
**Area: 20,000 m²**
**Further participants:**
**East China Architectural Design & Research Institute, Mindscape, Studio Taximizu, Md. Design, Interdesign Associates**
**Technical features:**
**Large green public space complex on the roof of Shanghai's central metro station.**

An urban green valley complex sits above one of Shanghai's busiest subway stations. The designers integrated a pedestrianized landscape park, which represents the project's most striking highlight. The 20,000-square-meter Greenland Center, devised in line with the URBAN FARM concept – fusing nature and human space – weaves through the intelligent roof geometry and into the residents' everyday city life. The roof is divided into a number of individual sections of different dimensions, connected at various heights. This results in a fascinating three-dimensional exterior platform and a slope, both of which are closely intermeshed and reflect the building's functions and the human activities taking place beneath the roof. The architectural topology takes the shape of a canyon with a building area of 300,000 square meters. The design envisages a wide stretch of landscape at the center of the site. Situated right across from Shanghai's central subway station, it attracts all those who use the station on a daily basis and the area's residents. Large green spaces are planned for the site, with many little places for activities scattered across the area at different elevations, inspired by a traditional element of Shanghai's architecture: the tiger window. The three-dimensional intertwining of all of these activity spaces creates a generous, green public area. The project fully exploits environmental technology by arranging all commercial routes in semi-covered rooms that don't require any climate control. This means that they can do without air-conditioning units, which reduces the project's annual $CO^2$ emissions by approximately 72,200 tons – equivalent to the amount of $CO^2$ absorbed by 26.2 hectares of forest.

Plants mainly used: trees, shrubs and grass.

*Top view of green roofs. Exterior view. View of the covered paths. View from above. Roof plan.*

Main view. View of green roof terraces from above.

# Index

AAFH!
www.aafh.be 84

Aidlin Darling Design
www.aidlindarlingdesign.com 24

ALH Taller
www.alhtaller.com 136

blrm Architekt*innen
www.blrm.eu 96

Byoung Cho / BCHO Partners
www.bchoarchitects.com 72

CHIO Architects (Singapore)
www.chioarchitects.sg 64

Cityplot
www.cityplot.org 156

DDconcept Architecture
facebook.com/ddconcept.vn 148

FAAB Architektura
www.faab.pl 48

Aleš Fiala
www.alesfiala.com
www.gurdau.com 160

Heatherwick studio
www.heatherwick.com 12

KANOPEA ARCHITECTURE STUDIO
www.kanopea-architecture-studio.com 120

Koichi Takada Architects
www.koichitakada.com 40

KRADS
www.krads.is 132

Landschaftsarchitektur+ Holzapfel-Herziger & Benesch
www.l-plus.de 16, 140

LAVA - Laboratory for Visionary Architecture
www.l-a-v-a.com 156

Matt Gibson Architecture & Design
www.mattgibson.com.au 144

MIA Design Studio
www.miadesignstudio.com 88

MVRDV
www.mvrdv.com 44

Hiroshi Nakamura & NAP
www.nakam.info 36

Nakshabid Architects
www.nakshabid.com 76

Nikken Sekkei
www.nikken.co.jp/ja 168

Perkins&Will
www.perkinswill.com 108

Pham Huu Son Architects
www.phsarchitects.net 52, 112

Phạm Thanh Truyền, Phún Bảo Long and Partners
www.catmoc.cmg.vn 164

Piuarch
www.piuarch.it 56

querkraft
www.querkraft.at 124

RATAPLAN - Architektur ZT
www.rataplan.at 104

Ana Ruivo, Baixo Impacto Arquitetura
www.arqbaixoimpacto.com.br 68

Ryuichi Ashizawa Architects & associates
www.r-a-architects.com 92

Aika Schluchtmann, Schluchtmann Architekten
www.schluchtmannpartner.de 116

Snøhetta
www.snohetta.com 28

Sou Fujimoto Architects
www.sou-fujimoto.net 8

Stefano Boeri Architetti
www.stefanoboeriarchitetti.net 152

Studio Paul Kaloustian
www.paulkaloustian.com 100

Studio Vural
www.studiovural.com 60

T3 ARCHITECTS
www.t3architects.com 120

TAA Design
www.taadesign.com 32

Tom Munz Architekt*innen
www.tommunz.com 80

Triptyque
www.triptyque.com 20

Wallflower Architecture + Design
www.wallflower.com.sg 128

# Picture Credits

| | |
|---|---|
| 9AM Arquitectura s.a.s | 136–139 |
| Adam Rouse Photography | 24–27 |
| Daici Ano + Tomoyuki Kusunose | 10 b. l. |
| Binyan Studios | 40–43 |
| Ladina Bischof | 80–83 |
| blrm | 96–99 |
| BoysPlayNice | 160–163 |
| Jakub Certowicz | 48–51 |
| Trieu Chien | 88–91 |
| City Syntax | 78 l. |
| Michel Denancé | 21, 22 a., 23 a. |
| Finbarr Fallon | 128–131 |
| Christian Flatscher | 28–31 |
| Christophe Haesevoets | 84–87 |
| Christina Häusler | 125, 126 l., 127 a. |
| Hiroshi Nakamura & NAP | 39 a. |
| Hu Wenjie | 168–171 |
| Hufton + Crow Photography | 12–15 |
| Hertha Hurnaus | 126 r., 127 b. |
| Kaori Ichikawa | 92–95 |
| Paul Kaloustian | 100–103 |
| Bayejid Mahbub Khondker | 76 b. |
| Landschaftsarchitektur+ | 140–143 |
| LAVA - Laboratory for Visionary Architecture with Cityplot | 156–159 |
| Hoang Le | 32–35 |
| Nic Lehoux | 108–111 |
| Marcello Mariana | 56–59 |
| Shannon McGrath | 144–147 |
| Yang Min (mintwow) | 168–171 |
| Yann Monel | 20, 22 b. r., 22 b. l., 23 b. |
| Giovanni Nardi | 152–155 |
| Hiroyuki Oki | 52–55, 112–115, 148–151 |
| Kohei Omachi | 37 r., 39 b. |
| Oolhar.co | 68–71 |
| Youngtae Park | 73 |
| Jeong Park | 75 a. |
| Paul Phan | 64–67 |
| Phú Đào studio | 164–167 |
| Sergio Pirrone | 72, 74, 75 b. |
| Junaid Hasan Pranto | 76 a., 78 r., 79 |
| querkraft-ZOOM VP | 124 |
| RATAPLAN | 104–107 |
| Schluchtmann Architekten | 116–119 |
| Shanghai Duying Cultural Communication Co., Ltd | 168–171 |
| Shephotoerd | 44–47 |
| Boris Storz | 6–7, 16–19 |
| Katsumasa Tanaka | 8, 9, 10 a., 10 b. r., 11 |
| Marino Thorlacius | 132–135 |
| Bruce Vincentiis | 120–123 |
| Dom Wipas | 60–63 |
| Yuka Yanazume | 37, 38 l. |

All other pictures were made available by the architects or designers.

Cover front: BoysPlayNice
Cover back (from left to right, from above to below): Katsumasa Tanaka, Shannon McGrath, Jakub Certowicz, Hoang Le, Bruce Vincentiis

# Imprint

The Deutsche Nationalbibliothek lists this publication in the Deutsche Nationalbiblio-grafie; detailed bibliographic data are available in the Internet at http://dnb.dnb.de

ISBN 978-3-03768-298-2

www.braun-publishing.ch



1st edition 2025

Editor: Sibylle Kramer
Editorial staff and layout: Alessia Calabrò
Translation: Anja Wiest
Graphic concept: Michaela Prinz, Berlin
Reproduction: Bild1Druck GmbH, Berlin



Product Safety
Publisher: Braun Publishing AG,
Arenenbergstr. 2, 8268 Salenstein, Switzerland,
publisher@braun-publishing.ch
EU-Representative: Bookwise GmbH,
Zeppelinstr. 67, 81669 Munich, Germany,
info@bookwise.de